The Golgotha Earthquake

The Golgotha Earthquake
Three Witnesses

Paul Sevier Minear

The Pilgrim Press
Cleveland, Ohio

The Pilgrim Press, Cleveland, Ohio 44115
© 1995 by Paul Sevier Minear

Biblical quotations are from the New Revised Standard Version of the Bible,
© 1989 by the Division of Christian Education of the National Council
of the Churches of Christ in the U.S.A., and are used by permission

Printed in the United States of America on acid-free paper

00 99 98 97 96 95   5 4 3 2 1

Library of Congress Cataloging-in-Publication Data

Minear, Paul Sevier, 1906–
The Golgotha earthquake : three witnesses / Paul Sevier Minear.
p.   cm.
Includes bibliographical references and index.
ISBN 0-8298-1070-6
1. Jesus Christ—Crucifixion—Biblical teaching.
2. Bible. N.T. Romans—Criticism, interpretation, etc.
3. Bible. N.T. Hebrews—Criticism, interpretation, etc.
2. Bible. N.T. Matthew—Criticism, interpretation, etc.   I. Title.
BT450.M53   1995
232.9'63—dc20
95-18071
CIP

To

Allan L. Toole, M.D.

Maryann Tranquilli, R.N.

whose pacemaker skills

have prolonged

my life

Contents

Prologue

The whole world is Calvary writ large . . .
A man's soul is Calvary writ small.[1]

All people die. The memory of most dies soon thereafter. One of those deaths, however, millions remember with gratitude every day. Other millions voice their gratitude every week with hymns and prayers. Most calendars issue an annual, though silent, call to remember. All this despite nineteen centuries, and more, that intervene. All this despite the manner of that death—crucifixion as an enemy of God and the people. Such was the death of Jesus, a prophet from Nazareth of Galilee, executed outside the walls of Jerusalem at the Place of the Skull, called Golgotha.

Those who commemorate Jesus' death do so because they find in it links to the story of all humankind, as the above epigraph suggests. This death did more than identify the origin of one of the world's religions—much more. It released the power and the wisdom of God in such a way as to destroy confidence in the power of human rulers and the wisdom of earth's wisest people. It disclosed the design of God's creative work at all times, inasmuch as "from him and through him and to him are all things." In that design millions of followers still discover elemental and universal significance. This significance is evidenced in the grateful testimony of three early

witnesses: the authors of the letters to the Romans and the
Hebrews and the Gospel of Matthew.

To emphasize the divine imprimatur on Jesus' death, two
of those authors employ the image of a shaking heaven and a
shaking earth. In the case of Matthew, the earthquake includes a darkness at noon followed by dawn in midafternoon,
a destroyed sanctuary and opened tombs, and a fear-driven
confession from the most unlikely source. While not incorpo-
rating the earthquake image, the third author's view of the
impact of God's action is no less radical. Their consensus in
viewing Jesus' death as the occasion when God disclosed
both final judgment and eternal mercy suggested to me the title of this book, *The Golgotha Earthquake.*

Just as my title points to such a consensus, the chapter
headings suggest varying perspectives and concerns. In the
case of Paul's letter to the Romans, the death of Jesus was an
event of atonement that marked an end to the age of sin and
death and a beginning to the age of forgiveness and life:

> The creation was subjected to futility [the old age] not of its
> own will but by the will of the one who subjected it, in hope
> that the creation will be set free from its bondage to decay
> and will obtain the freedom of the glory of the children of
> God [the new age]. (Rom. 8:20–21)

Chapter 1, therefore, explores the thinking of the apostle concerning the new creation.

The anonymous author of the letter to the Hebrews focuses attention not so much on the two ages as on the two
covenants between God and God's people, one covenant
sealed on Mount Sinai and the other on Mount Zion. But the
range of the writer's concern is no more limited than Paul's.
Appealing for a precedent to the account of Cain's murder of
Abel (Gen. 4:1–16), this witness recalls how God had accepted
the offering of one brother but rejected the offering of the other.
This rejection led to Cain's violent act; when the earth drank

Abel's blood, it called out for God to take vengeance against the elder brother. So when God speaks through the blood of Jesus, creating a new covenant in that blood, both the heavens and the earth shake. The outcome is a form of offering, of worship, that replaces all earlier patterns and forms. Chapter 2 explores this author's thinking concerning the new worship.

The Gospel of Matthew illustrates a different form of writing, in which the concerns and perspectives of the anonymous author must be inferred from the way in which the oral and written traditions about Jesus are organized and interpreted. To Matthew, the execution of Jesus on Golgotha is a fulfillment of his vocation as God's Son, and the character of that vocation is clearly embodied in stories of his teachings, his healings, his ministry to his people, and his controversies with their leaders. To Matthew, it is the fulfillment of that vocation that leads inexorably and by God's design to Jesus' rejection by his people, his crucifixion, and his resurrection. Moreover, this complex tradition about Jesus' vocation provides essential clues to the vocation of those whom Jesus chooses to continue his work. Accordingly, chapter 3 explores the dimensions of this shared vocation: like master, like servants.

It must be admitted that none of these three authors was present at the Place of the Skull on the first Good Friday. That fact may weaken their testimony for those who require impeccable and impartial observers of any historical event. In this case, however, no report from firsthand observers has survived, and we must therefore do the best we can with what remains. These three had become familiar with the earliest traditions of the event. They had experienced violent conflicts similar to those that had erupted in crucifixion. A still greater authenticity is conferred on their reports by their earlier disposition (like Paul's) to agree with Jesus' adversaries before their minds were decisively transformed by the event itself. Contrary to this previous disposition, their perceptions of the world had been revolutionized: ideas about life and its hidden origins, about death and its equally hidden finalities, about society and its false certainties, about power and its deceptive efficacies. All had been changed.

The validity of their witness is supported above all by the fact that all three had accepted a calling from the Crucified himself, a calling that required them to carry their own cross. In their view, Jesus' approval of their work took priority over the verdict of any other judge. Their critics have long been embarrassed by such evidence of their trustworthiness. Their witness to Golgotha left open only two options—to trust them or to trust their enemies. The event was of such a character as to exclude any third option. Ever since, their credibility and authority have been recognized by virtually all Christians and even by many who have belied their calling.

Initially, I had begun to explore these writers' thought from angles other than their witness to Golgotha. In the case of Paul's letter to the Romans, my concern originally centered on chapter 13, which has become a favorite tool of Christians for supporting highly reactionary politics:

> Let every person be subject to the governing authorities, for there is no authority except from God. . . . Whoever resists authority resists what God has appointed and those who resist will incur judgment. (13:1–2)

The appeal to this text to support the desire of the "Christian right" to wield governmental power represents one of the most amazing reversals in history. Paul addresses his teaching to a tiny cluster of Christian communes that were being violently persecuted by the governing authorities. They had no possibility of exerting any political clout. Yet this text has been turned into ammunition for power-seeking reactionaries in our day, who appeal to Romans to justify political idolatries. Thus, my study began in an effort to understand how Paul's radical thinking about Jesus the criminal could have become the ideological base for such idolatries.

In the case of Hebrews, my interest initially grew out of another apparent reversal of scriptural radicalism. How did Jesus' vicarious death become the ideological base for a new priesthood that demanded "high church" liturgical routines and ecclesiastical subservience? The vocabulary is admittedly priestly and sacrificial: "We have a great high priest who has passed through the heavens . . . " (4:14). "He holds his priesthood permanently because he continues forever. . . . He is able for all time to save those who approach God through him" (7:24–25). "He entered heaven itself, now to appear in the presence of God on our behalf" (9:24). "By a single offering he has perfected for all time those who are sanctified" (10:14). All these images of blood, of sacrifices, of sanctification, and of the priesthood seem to many interpreters not only to justify but to require monopolistic conceptions of salvation, controlled by a new institution of ecclesiastical and liturgical authority. This question, then, seems to require an answer: how did the new covenant in Jesus' blood, as witnessed in this letter, come to support institutions even more monopolistic and more exclusive than the temple and priesthood in Jesus' day?

In the case of Matthew, another perverse kind of scriptural interpretation calls for examination. Chapter 24 of the Gospel, the so-called Little Apocalypse, has been used in recent days to justify a radical sectarianism that capitalizes on its own interpretation of the end of the world. Readers will recall Jonestown and the more recent Waco community. Their position seems no more eccentric or fantastic than this prediction: "Then the sign of the Son of Man will appear in heaven, and then all the tribes of earth will mourn, and they will see the Son of Man coming on the clouds of heaven with power and great glory" (Matt. 24:30). That Christians should expect such a sign and that scripture requires them to expect it are standard convictions in current sectarianism—convictions that have jeopardized respect for the Gospel itself. Such sectarianism has prompted me to look again at the initial linkage between the death of Jesus and this extremist fantasy.

As I pursued these separate projects, they converged more and more into a single study of the impact of the Golgotha event on the basic outlook of these three thinkers. On one hand, all three believed that God had introduced a new age, a renewal of creation unparalleled in range since the sin and death of Adam and Eve. On the other hand, their witness has become a sacred scripture used to validate a reactionary political ethic, a highly routinized liturgical and priest-centered ecclesiasticism, and a radical apocalyptic sectarianism—all exploiting, in various ways, the Passion story of Jesus.

The conflict between scripture and these perversions of it posed a question for me that I could not ignore: as a veteran interpreter of the New Testament, recognizing these interpretations of the new creation as betrayals, would I do nothing to present an alternative interpretation of the Golgotha earthquake? My three chapters offer an answer. Yet this has now become a secondary objective, my primary objective being a clearer comprehension of the new creation, the new worship, and the new vocation.

The New Revised Standard Version of the Bible provides the text for these studies, although occasionally I use my own translation. In its translation of the biblical authors, the NRSV rightly uses masculine metaphors when these authors speak of God or the Messiah: Father, Son, Lord, King. When I comment on texts where these metaphors appear, I would introduce both linguistic and theological confusion were I to substitute inclusive-language metaphors. As their interpreter and spokesman, I am honor-bound to respect the thought of the ancient authors; modern readers owe them the same respect. Honesty demands that we be content with nothing less.

1

The Letter to the Romans: A New Creation

God's glory is a wondrous thing,
Most strange in all its ways,
And, of all things on earth, least like
What men agree to praise.[1]

Nowhere does Paul use the term *earthquake;* nor does the place name *Golgotha* appear in his letters. Nevertheless, few writers in the vast literature of the church speak more frequently of Jesus' death by crucifixion or of the divine power which that death released. No biographer of Paul can fail to tell of the radical uprooting in his life that Jesus' death produced. He became convinced that no event since the creation of Adam had marked so great a change in God's mode of governing the world. The wisdom of the cross had reduced to folly the wisdom of the wisest; the power of the cross had reduced to impotence the strength of the strongest. By the cross, God had "reduced to nothing the things that are" (1 Cor. 1:18–29). What earthquake could be more devastating? The cross demanded new ways of seeing, thinking, and acting if people were to cope with God's complete restructuring of their world. Paul's letters provide our earliest documentary witness to such a reconstruction.

A Starting Point

Let me start with an axiom that serves as a premise for all of Paul's thinking, a conviction that marks his mind as profoundly theocentric. This axiom serves as a fitting summary of the first eleven chapters of Romans as well as a preface to the rest of the letter.

> From him [God] and through him and to him are all things.
> To him be the glory forever! Amen. (Rom. 11:36)

No words could better express the motivation of this thinker than this ascription of all glory to God. No words could more concisely circumscribe the map of the world within which he lived than those three prepositional phrases. Those three prepositions—*from, through, to*—or their equivalents appear to be essential in every human language. Of course, they are commonly used very casually, by people talking about daily occurrences, unaware of any more profound importance. In this instance, however, they embrace the origins, the means of sustenance, and the outcomes of all human stories. The dimensions of this thought-world are universal as well as personal, ultimate as well as intimate. Paul could imagine nothing as falling outside the range of those three phrases. They assumed the unlimited primacy of God and asserted an absolute priority for God's purposes and designs. Every human desire and action, however trivial or influential, channeled the hidden operation of those purposes. Given that, it is not surprising that those three prepositions dominate the texture of all of Paul's thinking.

From him applied to every instance of wrath or mercy (11:32), every authority operating in human society (13:2), and every gift of grace (12:6). *To him* indicated the motivation of every sacrifice (12:2), the orientation of the bowed knee (14:11), and the consummation of all glory, human or divine (11:36).

Through him established firm bonds between what God has done, is doing, and will do and every human action, however evil or good. God's powerful purposes, dependent on none other, were declared to be active throughout the whole of creation, nonhuman as well as human. For Paul, this included all that God intended to do *through* Jesus Christ, the Firstborn. So oriented, human thought was so inclusive as to stun the imagination.

Can anyone truly think about all things as examples of this *from-through-to* syndrome? Can anyone think *with* Paul, so completely entering his God-talk as to grasp how he thought and why he thought as he did?[2] Many students doubt it. For them H. K. McArthur speaks: "It is impossible for a modern Western person to think and feel in the categories of the first century, whether those of the Palestine world or the larger Hellenistic World."[3] I am not so sure of this impossibility as is McArthur. Surely Paul expected some of his readers in Rome to be able to think *with* him about God. And what he supposed was possible for them may not be wholly beyond our grasp if we make the requisite effort and accept the daunting risks. Paul was well aware, of course, of the difficulties in asserting knowledge of God:

> how unsearchable are his judgments
> and how inscrutable his ways,
> for who has known the mind of the Lord
> or who has been his counselor? (11:33–34)

Did Paul forget this inscrutability, or had the gospel actually disclosed to him the ways of the Creator? If the latter, can Paul relay to us, in turn, his understanding of those ways? Such questions are not easy to answer.

A first step will be to recognize one characteristic of Paul's thinking, which he held in common with Jesus and the other apostles. Their thinking about God's ways in creation was so patterned as to distinguish two modes of divine government, in both modes of which human actions were interpreted as simultaneously expressing the convergence of divine prevenience and human choices. Usually this characteristic has been called Paul's penchant for two-age thinking, distinguishing God's mode of governing the old age from God's mode of governing the new: "Paul's two-age thinking shapes the way he thinks and does not think about significant issues, and this is the case precisely when he does not refer explicitly to the two-age schema."[4] If in our reading of Romans we can grasp his understanding of the *from-through-to* patterns in each of the two ages, we will be able to move much closer to our goal. Fortunately, Paul has furnished us with clues to the boundaries between these two ages. These boundaries are not defined chronologically, by reference to a date on the timeline, but theologically, by reference to the *from-through-to* dimensions in the Creator's design. We will now explore four examples of two-age thinking.

The Age of Wrath/The Age of Grace (Chapters 1–4)

In Paul's first chapters, he concentrates on describing the ways in which God had dealt with two major segments of humanity: the Gentiles and the Jews. Both had lived in an age that began in God's wrath and ended in God's wrath. To both, the knowledge of God had been so accessible that both had been "without excuse" (1:20) for defying it. In both cases, it was the gospel that had disclosed God's wrath. Such wrath was at once self-chosen and God-intended.

Paul describes the rebellion of Gentiles and Jews in different ways, though he makes exceptions for individual Gentiles (1:14, 27) and Jews (2:13). His picture of Gentile heartlessness and ruthlessness is vivid enough to please any misanthrope. The Gentiles had exchanged God's truth for a lie and had refused to acknowledge or be thankful for God's gifts in creation. Blessed by the knowledge of God's accessibility in creation, they had refused to accept God as the One from whom and to whom are all things. Because of their ingratitude, God had "given them up" to "a debased mind and to things that should not be done" (1:24). Claiming to act independently, their very claim coincided with God's wrath in "giving them up" to an existence ruled by their self-interest: the age of wrath.

Then, speaking as a Jew to Jews, Paul describes their situation in no less austere terms. God showed the Jews no partiality, although their actions indicated that they thought otherwise. Like Gentiles, they had access to knowledge of God through all creation. They had also known God through the law, which had only confirmed them in their sin. In judging Gentiles as inferior, they invoked God's judgment on themselves. By ungrateful and impenitent hearts, they signaled their own alienation from God, so that in claiming to be the chosen people and therefore superior to the Gentiles, they had blasphemed God before those very Gentiles. Minds thus ruled by God's wrath had stored up wrath for the coming day of wrath, when God would judge "the secret sins of all" (2:16). The age of wrath was thus coterminous with all who lived under the power of sin (3:9), all who fell short of God's glory (3:23), all for whom ingratitude perverted grace into alienation.

To describe the unity of Gentiles and Jews in the age of wrath, Paul had recourse to a collage of citations from the Psalms (Rom. 3:10–18). He seems to have chosen these citations (from at least six different psalms) because they resonate with God's archetypal curses in Genesis 3 and 4. Their reliance on lies, "the venom of vipers under their lips," suggests that they were offspring of the first liar, the serpent (Gen. 3:12). Their swiftness in shedding blood recalls the first fratricide. The image of throats as opened graves smells of God's promise of death to Adam. Paths full of "ruin and misery" describe God's curse on the earth, while ignorance of "the way of peace" presupposes eviction from paradise. It was thus, according to Paul, that God had held the whole world accountable (Rom. 3:19)—so inclusive and so desolate was the age of wrath.

This long elaboration of the life ruled by this conjunction of God's wrath and human ingratitude led Paul to a brief declaration of the stark contrasts that the new age promised (3:21–31). This age was ruled by the gift of God's grace, a gift that God had made through "the redemption that is in Christ Jesus." Through the blood of Christ (the term *blood* may have been intended as a counterforce to the blood shed by Cain, as in Heb. 12:24), God had put forward "a sacrifice of atonement" that had become "effective *through* faith" (all uses of this crucial preposition should be noted). That faith, in turn, had established a law that excluded all boasting on the part of recipients. The righteousness of God had declared as righteous all those who had faith in Jesus. It was thus that the Creator had taken the initiative in creating an age ruled by grace/faith to replace the age of rebellion/wrath.

In this very brief paragraph, Paul summarizes the essential components of the life that is governed by grace: God's gracious intent and righteousness, the death of Jesus as a place of atonement, the faith *of* Christ Jesus embedded in that death, faith *in* that sacrifice, the righteousness of that faith, the new gratitude, the replacement of human boasting by human sharing in God's glory. *From* grace . . . *through* atonement . . . *to* glory.

This series of assertions, however, aroused deep resistance among many Jewish Christians who opposed Paul's insistence that there was no distinction in culpability between Gentiles who sinned apart from the law and Jews who sinned under the law. They could not agree that God's blessing of both groups eliminated their own right to boast of God's gift of the law. They believed that Paul's position was tantamount to overthrowing the law. "On the contrary," Paul writes, "we uphold the law" (3:31). He shows how that is true by appealing to the very ancestor in whose story God had disclosed Israel as the chosen people. Paul's opponents believed that in choosing Abraham as the father of Israel, God had required circumcision as a sign of such intention and that, therefore, obedience to this requirement formed the boundary between God's elect people and all others. The issue became one of priority: had God declared Abraham righteous before or after he had been circumcised? Paul insists that it was before. In his defense of this position, Paul appeals to many *befores:* before circumcision, righteousness and blessedness; before righteousness, faith; before faith, God's promise; before that promise, God's purpose; before that purpose, God's grace— the powerful grace of One who "gives life to the dead and calls into existence the things that do not exist" (4:17). All of these were infallible marks of a new creation. The faith of Abraham, as recorded in the law, confirmed the faith of both Jewish and Gentile believers in the God who had raised Jesus from the dead (4:24–25).

Paul's argument has two corollaries of some importance for our later study. First, in this context, the term *age* is measured not by successive epochs marked out on a single timeline but by the power that exercised dominion over human hearts. Second, the term *wrath* does not connote a vindictive emotion of anger on God's part; rather it describes the heartless and hopeless existence on the part of human creatures who have no excuse for their guilt, having known God's goodness before choosing to live "under the power of sin."

Death in Adam/Life in Christ (Chapters 5–6)

The chain of *befores* that underlies Paul's argument about Abraham makes one particular link essential: "the redemption that is in Jesus" (3:24; 4:24–25). In chapter 5 Paul examines that link more closely. In this new context, the place of atonement marks the boundary between the age of Adam and the age of Christ or, to avoid the error of chronological measurement, between a mind ruled by the law of sin-and-death and a mind ruled by the law of the Spirit of life (8:1).

In a few terse declarations, Paul outlines the map of the new world of faith. *From* God comes "access to this grace in which we stand." Such access is opened "*through* our Lord Jesus Christ." Accordingly, hope is born, the hope "of sharing the glory of God." The immediate ground of such hope is the love poured into hearts "*through* the Holy Spirit" (5:5). Assurance of rescue from the age of death is implicit in the fact that Christ died for residents of that age while they were weak—sinners and enemies of God. Love as demonstrated by that death so established a new *origin* that it produced a new *end:* "salvation by his life." The new chain of *beforenesses,* as in the case of Abraham, created a new humanity for which the only adequate analogy is God's creation of Adam. "Adam exchanged his share in divine glory for slavery to sin and death. Christ changed places with this Adam, sharing Adam's subjection to sin and death in order that Adam might experience Christ's victory over sin and death."[5]

Sin had come through Adam's misguided defiance of God's command; through that sin death had come, extending its dominion over all. In tracing this contrary chain of beforenesses, Paul's thought was clearly shaped by the Genesis story, which sets the conditions that the new age had replaced; it does this by describing the from-through-to syndrome of life lived under the law of sin and death. "Just as sin exercised dominion in death, so grace might also exercise dominion through justification leading to eternal life through Jesus Christ our Lord" (5:21). Thus, in chapter 5 Paul invites readers to press behind the inherited distinctions between Jews and Gentiles, even behind any historical religious system of law and ritual, back to their primal bond with their Creator and to their eviction from paradise, where everything had been "very good." The age of wrath had its ultimate origin in the sin of Adam, through human ingratitude and self-will.

But the contrast between death in Adam and life in Christ provides something more than a way of accenting the importance of Christ's death in opening the way for the reconciliation of God's enemies. To be sure, the death of Christ had accomplished this miraculous revolution in human affairs: "Just as by the one man's disobedience, the many were made sinners, so by the one man's obedience, the many will be made righteous" (5:19). That very act of obedience, however, demonstrates this essential corollary: "the many" who had thus been made righteous were enlisted in that very work of reconciliation; they were called to share in the death through which the gift of life had come. They had died to sin. They had been baptized into Christ by being baptized into his death. Their old Adamic self had been crucified with him and thus freed from sin. Now that God's grace had established its dominion over them, they must reject any relapse into slavery to sin. The boundary between being dead in Adam and being alive to God in Christ was a boundary they must cross daily by dying to the dominion of death (6:1–14).

We may summarize this second illustration of two-age thinking by stressing two ways in which Paul's thinking marks an advance over that of the first illustration. Because Adam was the first human being, death in Adam connotes a dominion even more inclusive than the realm of sins shared by Jews and Gentiles. To say "Adam" is to say "Everyone." By the same token, life in Christ establishes an even more radical demand on all recipients: they must choose to die daily to the dominion of death. To say "Christ" is also to say "Everyone."

Creation Bound/Creation Freed (Chapters 7–8)

In chapter 7 Paul describes the long battle between living in the flesh as slaves to sin and living in the Spirit. That battle reached a climax in an anguished cry: "Wretched man that I am! Who will rescue me from this body of death?" (7:24). That cry emerged from a continuing struggle between the mind enslaved to the law of God and the flesh enslaved to the law of sin. Believers had fixed their minds on things of the Spirit and were no longer in the flesh. Yet at the same time, this whole letter is an appeal to readers *not* to live as debtors to the flesh, as slaves to its commands (8:12). To understand Paul's view of the two modes of government, therefore, readers must comprehend the full scope of "the body of death" that was constituted by minds set on the flesh, "sold into slavery to sin (7:14). Only then can they fully grasp the dimensions of the rescue and its resulting freedom.

The struggle with the body of death which individual believers experience, according to chapter 7, is linked in Paul's mind to the agony of the whole creation, as described in chapter 8. Each individual's slavery to sin constitutes participation in creation's slavery to decay. Such decay, such a body of death, points back to God's initial curse on Adam and Eve, in Genesis 3. Since then the creation has been groaning in labor pains. That metaphor of labor pains echoes God's curse on Eve as penalty for her gullibility to the serpent's seduction and her desire for fruit from the tree of knowledge. So, too, the futility of creation recalls God's curse on the earth, with its long harvest of thorns and thistles, its stubborn resistance to the farmer's desires for survival and security. "The body of death" also resonates with memories of the endless story of brutality and bloodshed flowing from Cain's resentment over God's preference for his younger brother's sacrifice. Most clearly, the agony of creation fulfills God's promise, "You will die." (What another Jew thought when he said "Adam" may be found in Sir. 40:1–11.)

Throughout chapter 8, then, Paul has in mind the long heritage of a cosmic "body of death," which recipients of the Spirit share: "we ourselves . . . groan inwardly [the same labor pains] while we wait for adoption, the redemption of our *body*" (8:23). Significantly, that noun *body* is singular, not plural. In Paul's view, the whole creation is a single unredeemed body of death which believers share. In waiting patiently for the redemption of "our body," their sufferings are, in fact, the labor pains of that creation. Their experience thus provides the second important connotation of the childbirth image: believers exist as God's advance assurance of the termination of creation's birth pangs and therefore of a hope that enables them to wait with patience for the completion of God's design.

We have thus far failed to comment on the central thrust of Paul's key assertion: "the creation was subjected to futility, not *of* its own will, but *by* the will of the one who subjected it, in hope that the creation itself will be set free . . . " (8:20). Before Adam's choice, God's plan! The Creator's design preceded the corruption of creation, the eviction from Eden, the sentence of death. Before any such thing had happened, God had had a design for both ages, the subjection to futility of the first and the freedom from bondage of the second. Both ages had emerged from God's intention and foreknowledge. Although God had sold humankind into slavery to sin (7:14) and subjected creation to futility, both of these actions had been motivated by hope—*God's* hope that could be realized only through those very "labor pains."

From the first it has been difficult for Paul's readers to follow his thinking here because it calls for a radical revision in attitudes toward God as Creator, toward God's activity in creation, and toward the Genesis accounts that influenced Paul so strongly. Paul read Genesis 1 not in terms of the *how* and the *when* of the action, but in terms of *who* and *why*. Who had commanded "Let there be light," and why? Who had issued the threat, "You will die," and why? What was the initial design, the strategic decisions, before the first word had been spoken? As Bishop Kenneth Cragg writes, "Intentionality, rather than mere beginning, is the meaning of creation, containing any question as to 'how' within the answer 'why.' "[6] It is the mystery of this intentionality that lies within and behind all other mysteries: "*From* him are all things." In Romans 8 Paul probes into this mystery in his effort to comprehend God's intention before Adam sinned.

One clue appears in the phrase "the Spirit of life" (8:1). Like many other early Christian writers, Paul associates the Holy Spirit with that wind or breath of God that had swept over the face of the waters (Gen. 1:2). Through that Spirit life had come into existence; the Spirit of life thus became an expression of the primal intention for all creation even before the creative word was spoken. For Paul that same Spirit of life, that same intentionality, was expressed through Jesus Christ. God's intention—that is, foreknowledge—had made Jesus God's Firstborn. That term *Firstborn* carries a double thrust: it points backward to the divine foreknowledge both before Adam and before the large family of siblings, whom God had foreknown and called according to his purpose (8:27–30). And it points forward to the predestination of this family "to be conformed to the image of his Son." God's primal purpose thus determined the destiny as well as the origin of this family. When they cried "Abba! Father!" the cry was the Holy Spirit's identification of them as "heirs of God and joint-heirs with Christ" (8:15–16). The "law of the Spirit of life in Christ Jesus" had thus freed these members of the family of the Firstborn from the law of sin and death; this freedom, in fact, had been the objective hidden within God's subjection of creation to that "body of death." It now became true of the firstborn children that "the body is dead because of sin, the Spirit is life because of righteousness" (8:10). Such for Paul became the basic vocabulary for speaking of the ultimate birth of the children of God: the Creator; God's purpose, Spirit, and life; God's foreknowledge and sending of this Son; the death and resurrection of this Son; the gift of the Spirit of life to the other children; and the walking by the Spirit through which these children disclosed their freedom from bondage to sin in the flesh. All these were part of Paul's vision of God's plan before God had subjected all things to the bondage of ultimate decay.

There is another feature in Paul's reading of God's plan before the age of wrath, before the labor pains of creation, and before the redemption of the body of death. Those destined to become heirs of God were also destined to become joint heirs with Christ through suffering with him (8:17). It was through such shared suffering that they would share in the labor pains of creation. Just as Jesus' acceptance of God's design had been embodied in his sufferings, so, too, Christ's love for others was embodied in their hardship, distress, persecution, famine, nakedness, peril, death (8:35). Only thus did those sufferings give a clear witness to God's hope for the whole of creation, the purpose hidden in its subjection to futility and in the gift of freedom from bondage to decay. Believers' hope for all creation thus became inseparable from confidence in their own justification and glorification (8:30). God's purpose for them became the ground of their hope for creation as a whole. That hope gave them power to wait patiently for the fulfillment of God's primal purpose, when through its labor pains, the creation would obtain the freedom of the glory of God's children (8:21). The parameters of Paul's thought thus include the widest conceivable horizons—a vision of the freedom of all creation embraced within the vision of God's primal design, a vision released by the love of God in Christ.

It must be admitted that Paul does not provide here a clear picture of how God would in the future transform the body of death. In 1 Cor. 15 Paul gives a clearer picture.[7] The picture that he gives in Romans is one of interpreting God's primal design, as disclosed in the accounts of creation and in the mission of Jesus, as well as one of action—the action of believers in voluntarily suffering with Christ and in thus demonstrating both the labor pains of creation and the freedom of the firstborn. In their experience at the interface between the two ages, they learned the truth that "suffering produces endurance, and endurance produces character, and character produces hope, and hope does not disappoint us . . ." (5:2–5). For Paul, such human hope is grounded in *God's* hope for creation (8:20). Between the human hope and God's primal act of hoping stretch a chain of verbal symbols, reaching back from human faith to God's word, foreknowledge, promise, and gracious intention for all creation. For Paul, each link in that chain of intentionality is secured by the inner presence of the Holy Spirit (v. 26), by the gift of God's Firstborn "for all of us" (v. 32), and by the discovery that sufferings shared with Christ Jesus assure a sharing in God's glory (vv. 17, 37). It is because faith is thus a response to God's gracious purpose in creating all things, that nothing whatever in that creation, "the body of death," can separate believers from that creative purpose (v. 39). The destiny of all creation was thus concealed within a divine design that had been disclosed in the good news of God's love in Christ.

Children of the Flesh/Children of the Promise (Chapters 9–11)

The first three illustrations of two-age thinking represent a steady increase in range and scope: from two divisions of humanity (Gentiles and Jews), to all descendants of Adam, and then to the body of flesh that binds human existence to the flesh of birds, beasts, and fish. The horizons of thought thus expanded until they extended from primal intention to final consummation. Within the scope of human history, those horizons ranged from Eden through Adam, Lot, Abraham, Jacob, Pharaoh, Moses, Isaiah and the other prophets, to the time of Paul's writing and the time when his letter was read in Rome. In chapters 9–11 Paul turns his attention to focus more narrowly on dilemmas both he and his readers in Rome were facing at the moment. Among those dilemmas was the hostility of many Jews, including at least some Jewish Christians, to Paul's version of the good news and its implications for faith.

The situation in Rome was one factor impelling Paul to shift his focus. Although he had never visited the several house-churches in Rome, chapter 16 indicates that he knew some of their members and leaders. He knew that some of those communes were embroiled in tense debates between those whom Paul called "the weak in faith" (including many Jews) and those whom he called "the strong in faith" (including many Gentiles). Such debates centered in whether believers should obey the scriptural demands regarding Sabbath observance and dietary restrictions, both of which were difficult to practice in a pagan world. Those debates had become so acute that common worship, including sacramental meals, had become virtually impossible. The longer these issues were debated, the less it became possible to achieve genuine reconciliation. To some believers in Rome, Paul's position as reported through various channels had probably become a source of increased confusion and animosity because it was not only extreme but also uncompromising. As he composed these chapters, he may well have been preparing to clarify his stance on these controversial issues, which he tackled directly in chapters 14–15. One reason for his concern stemmed from his plans to use Rome as base for an extended mission to Spain, for which he would need solid support from the Roman congregations.

Before then, of course, Paul was planning a trip to Jerusalem, accompanying a relief fund for impoverished believers. He hoped that these Jewish congregations, which were under constant pressure from their compatriots, would welcome such help, even though it came from Gentile sources. What was certain for Paul on his arrival in Jerusalem was a very hostile reception from Jewish opponents. Only a few years earlier, Paul had been one of their colleagues, charged by the high priest with the task of destroying the church. He knew the full weight of Jewish hostility to the followers of this crucified, and therefore discredited, Messiah. Now he would appear in Jerusalem as the chief exponent of that Messiah, devoted to breaking down the walls between Israel and the Gentiles. Now he was viewed as a chief enemy of Israel, venturing with his sedition into the holy city and the holy temple. It is understandable that he urged the Roman Christians to pray for him on that dangerous journey.

These chapters (9–11) respond in detail to some of the charges against Paul's position by these former colleagues who had become bitter enemies. They argue that, according to Paul, the word of God to Israel had failed and God's promises to Abraham and his descendants had become null and void (9:6–8). If the "purpose of election" on which Paul's gospel depends had failed in the case of God's election of Israel, no one should trust Paul's claims for God's election of this Messiah and his followers. If, as Paul announces, God had rejected Israel in favor of lawless Gentiles, such a betrayal would be rank injustice by God, which would be quite inconceivable. A God whose plan from the first had been to destroy Israel should not find fault with Israel for its acts of disobedience. A Messiah who had been, as Paul insists, "the end of the law" could not be the Messiah whose coming Israel awaited. If this Messiah had abrogated the law, then God was free at any time to revoke all other gifts and callings. Such a God could no longer be trusted to stand by any promises.

Paul uses these three chapters to disavow these charges. His adversaries having impugned his personal integrity, Paul defends his honesty by an appeal to his conscience, which he asserts is supported by the Holy Spirit, the ultimate test of truth in the new creation. No one could challenge his credentials as a loyal Jew; he was a descendant of Abraham, a member of one of the twelve tribes, one who belonged to the remnant of Israel which had been "chosen by grace" in fulfillment of God's promise to the prophets. Paul concedes to his enemies (some of whom, as a former Pharisee, he probably knew intimately) that to them belonged "the adoption, the glory, the covenants, the giving of the law, the worship and the promises" (9:4). His sadness over their rejection of the Messiah is so intense that, if it were possible, he would for their sake be "cut off from Christ" (9:3). Paul commends his enemies for their "zeal for God," however unenlightened, and assures them of his prayers for their salvation. The intensity of his argument shows how deeply their hostility disturbs him.

He realizes, of course, that the issues are too basic to be resolved by an appeal to his personal integrity. The chasm between him and these former colleagues could be bridged only by carefully phrased arguments appealing to a norm of authority that they would recognize. This required constant reference to God's self-revelation in the law and the prophets; this explains why he refers so frequently in these three chapters to explicit quotations from scripture. Moreover, in most of these citations, God speaks in the first person to Israel as to God's elect nation concerning the divine purposes for and through them. Such appeals to scripture are grounded in Paul's conviction that "the gifts and the calling of God are irrevocable" (11:29), a conviction on which he and his adversaries could agree. For Paul those gifts and that calling had been God's intention before the foundation of the world.

As Paul unfolds his argument concerning God's prevenient will, he speaks of the creation of two distinct families, the children of the flesh and the children of the promise (9:8). Although Paul's argument is too complex for us to retrace step by step, we may summarize the differences between the two families by a list of descriptive and definitive phrases.

The children of the flesh are:

a people with blinded eyes, deafened ears, hardened
     hearts,
heirs of God's curse on the earth,
recipients of the judgment on Sodom and Gomorrah,
those children of Sarah and Rebecca whom God hated,
the objects of God's wrath made for destruction,
those who rely on righteousness based on law,
those who seek a righteousness based on works,
the branches of the olive tree broken off because of un-
     belief,
God's enemies, whom God treated severely,
those who stumble over the stone laid by God,
a disobedient and stubborn people.

The children of the promise are:

children of God, called, elect, foreknown,
recipients of God's mercy and compassion,
true descendants of Abraham and Sarah, Isaac and
     Rebecca,
those obedient to the word of God and/or the word of
     Christ,
a remnant of Israel, chosen by grace,
Jewish recipients of "life from the dead,"
Gentiles, "not my people called my people,"
all the disobedient who now receive mercy,
all who call on the name of the Lord and are saved,
all who believe in the good news with their hearts,
the heirs of God's glory.

Paul supports these descriptions of both families by
specific allusions to scripture and through scripture to the
Creator's prevenient purposes before the "birth" of the two
families. To understand the relation of those purposes of God
to human choices and purposes, we need to penetrate the in-

ner logic of several key figures of speech. Paul selects from scripture four key figures: the potter and the clay; the stone and its human effects; the olive tree and its branches; and the hardening and opening of human hearts. Each of these scriptural images can produce confusion or illumination. In visualizing them, one should try to recover the reasoning that induced Paul to use them and not hold Paul responsible for later caricatures. The misleading implications of one image may be corrected by looking for the meanings common to all.

The analogy of the potter shaping clay utensils (9:19–21) is clearly meant to emphasize the priority of the potter's purpose in determining the variety of artifacts. A potter has every right to consider the function of each product before approaching the wheel, whether the vessel is intended to be a cherished work of art or a water jug for daily use. The clay is in no position to choose in advance what sort of utensil it is to become or to complain in retrospect about the potter's choice. The issue is whether potters can be trusted to make objects of usefulness in line with their own purpose. In the case of the divine potter, the primal purpose is to display "the riches of his glory for the objects of mercy." That purpose dictates all the uses of the clay.

In some respects, Paul's use of the stone image is quite different, although it illustrates a similar kind of thinking on his part, together with the intentions of the prophets whom he cites (9:30–10:4). Here Paul refers more explicitly to recent responses to the gospel message. By sending the Messiah to Israel, God laid a stone in Zion; that stone, fulfilling the prior intention, had produced two reactions, both intended by God and both predicted in scripture (see below, p. 75). Some people stumbled over the stone (presumably these were potential residents of Zion who had tried to secure righteousness by works that fulfilled the law) and had therefore rejected God's messenger. The same stone led others to faith in God's Messiah and to the righteousness that God gave on the basis of such faith. The stumbling of the one group brought riches to the faithful. This unintended result on the part of the stumblers, through the faith of the other group, promised an ultimate inclusion even for those who had stumbled (11:12). Thus God's grace would in the end be extended to all.

The farmer's care of the olive tree is a figure used to illustrate what had recently happened in the diverse responses to the gospel (11:17–24). This allegory portrays God as a farmer, primarily interested in the productivity of the tree which the farmer has planted with "a rich root." Now, as Jews had rejected God's purposes and Gentiles had accepted them, the farmer was engaged in pruning out unproductive branches and in grafting in their place branches from "a wild olive shoot." This pruning and grafting work demonstrates both severity and kindness. However, Paul's analogy defies both natural law and agricultural practice: in his concern to show the priority of kindness over severity, Paul pictures the farmer doing what no real farmer would ever do—grafting back onto the tree a dead branch that had previously been pruned away (11:23). Paul only wanted to show the importance of the bond between branch and tree. Only faith creates the bond to the tree and its root, and that faith appears in the form of an awe that destroys pride and a gratitude that eliminates presumption. Paul was not interested in legislating a universal law of the double predestination of individuals to eternal damnation or salvation; rather, his concern was to call attention to ways in which God's grace for both Jews and Gentiles was being demonstrated by diverse responses to the gospel, whether negative or positive.

Paul draws his fourth analogy from a favorite motif in scriptural prophecies. Many prophets had protested Israel's hardness of heart and had attributed those hardened hearts simultaneously to human stubbornness and to God's prevenient action. Having inherited that tradition, Paul uses it to good effect (11:7–10). So, at the time of Israel's initial emancipation, God had hardened the heart of Pharaoh "for the very purpose of showing my power in you" (9:9–10). Paul detects a similar intention among Jewish responses to the gospel. God had so planted the word in some hearts that they believed with the heart and were saved (10:10). The same word, however, had disclosed among others "a disobedient and contrary people" (10:21). Their hardened heart indicated that God had blinded their eyes and deafened their ears "down to this very day" (11:7). Although this hardening on the part of Israel had made them enemies of God, it had also enabled God to show divine mercy to Gentiles—a development which, in turn, had constituted a promise that God would take away Israel's sins so that "all Israel will be saved" (11:25–28). Thus the apostle defends both the irreversible character of God's calling and the primacy of God's grace. All had been enemies of God. As children of the flesh, they had become evidence of divine justice, examples of divine power, and heirs of wrath. But as children of the promise, all had become heirs of an ultimate mercy.

> God has imprisoned all in disobedience,
> so that he may have mercy on all. (11:32)

Those two lines epitomize the two-age thinking that permeates earlier chapters of the letter. We may now turn to a more detailed analysis of Paul's description of the new age, the age created by God's mercy.

Therefore . . . a Living Sacrifice

> I appeal to you therefore, brothers and sisters, by the mercies of God, to present your bodies as a living sacrifice, holy and acceptable to God, which is your reasonable service. (12:1)

These two verses are so strategic to everything that follows that they demand detailed analysis. Paul bases all subsequent demands on this initial *therefore*. When lightning flashes, thunder is therefore to be expected. What, in this case, is the lightning? Surely it is the mercies of God that Paul had just been describing, mercies that had, by God's design, reached each group of recipients through former enemies, Gentiles through Jews, Jews through Gentiles. Those mercies had repaired divisions that had been among the oldest and deepest among mortals. Those same mercies had provided the mysterious pivot in all the earlier examples of two-age thinking. Accordingly, Paul carefully shapes his entire argument, from 1:14 on, in such a way as to endow this *therefore* with maximum force. He also plans the later chapters to show the logical consequences of that earlier argument, the thunder to its lightning. God's mercies had represented the intentionality of the Creator of all things; what follows that *therefore* represents the thunder, the consummation of divine creativity through the recipients of those mercies. The will of this heavenly Father has come to fruition through the wills of those who cry "Abba! Father!" By using this *therefore,* Paul seeks to convey the strongest possible motivation for readers to accept his appeal. Few uses of this *therefore* could carry greater weight, whether in rhetorical terms or in terms of human action. All that later readers came to call Paul's theology is encapsulated in those mercies of God, those *beforenesses* in the Creator's design. By the same token, all that later came to be called Paul's ethics is comprised in the *afternesses* of that same *therefore*—all the human responses to those mercies. Together, the *befores* and the *afters* constituted the new age as government by God's grace.

The first of these *afters* is, in fact, an epitome of them all—the presentation of bodies as living sacrifices. Just as God's creative mercies had been disclosed in the redemption in Christ Jesus, "a place of atonement by his blood" (3:25), so this presentation on their part had become the "reasonable" way by which they would worship and serve the Creator. It is significant that Paul stresses the sacrifice of their *bodies*, having prepared for that emphasis by showing that these bodies linked them to the body of sin and death shared by all descendants of Adam and Eve. Furthermore, these bodies had constituted their solidarity with the body of flesh that united humankind to the birds, beasts, and fish; this body shared the futility of all creation. When believers had died with Christ, they had experienced the birth pangs of freedom from the bonds of sin and death. When they had been crucified with him, the body of sin had been destroyed and slavery to futility terminated (6:5–11). By dying, Jesus had made this form of worship, as Paul said, "reasonable," as reasonable as the bond between Cain's murder of Abel and all subsequent forms of hatred and violence.

Equally significant was Paul's labeling of this sacrifice as *living*. The precedent in Christ's sacrifice justified this term *living* in that it marked both the surrender of life and the creating of life: death in one language and life in another, death in one age and life in another. The holiness of the action was assured by the fact that it was nothing less than the human embodiment of God's mercies. Such worship was certain to be acceptable to God.

The next verse employs another idiom in describing the same transmutation of divine mercies into human self-sacrifice:

> Do not be conformed to this age, but be transformed by the renewal of your minds, so that you may discern what is the good and acceptable and perfect will of God. (12:2)

Here, by marking the boundary between the two ages, Paul shows how believers moved from one to the other. Both exit and entrance are described as located within the decisions made by human minds. As the old age was identified by the conformation of minds to it, exit from it and entrance into a new age were signaled by the renewal of those minds. Such renewal (a new creation!) proceeded through the channeling of divine mercies into human self-sacrifice, enabling former conformists to the will of "this age" to discern for the first time what all along had been the intentionality of the Creator. Minds so renewed considered themselves "dead to sin and alive to God in Christ Jesus" (6:11). Minds that judged all human actions by the mercies of God could tell which actions were good as judged by God's primal purpose; those actions freed creation (the old age) from its futility. It is such actions that Paul describes in the remaining chapters of Romans. In those chapters he is concerned with four behavioral areas: (1) with maintaining the internal unity of the "one body in Christ" (12:3–13); (2) with Christians' obligations to their persecutors (12:14–21); (3) with their duties toward civil magistrates and rulers (13:1–14); and (4) with internal disputes among Christians over the continued authority of the Mosaic laws on the Sabbath and on dietary restrictions (14:1–15:13). We will now briefly consider the first two and then scrutinize the third more fully.

Therefore . . . One Body in Christ (12:3–13)

This first example of Paul's ethical teaching is embodied in more than a dozen axioms that describe the inner life of the community of God's elect. Paul views different types of behavior as determined and empowered by varying gifts of God's grace and by different measures of faith. These behavior patterns all exemplify the chain of creativity that discloses God's intentionality. This cumbersome word indicates that God's intention is not perceived as a single one-time purpose, limited to the moment of inception and viewed apart from its consequences. Rather, it is viewed in terms of the entire chain of creative activity, extending from the original design to its final consummation; from God's grace and foreknowledge through the divine plan for the two ages (the first as a necessary prelude to the second), to the election of the firstborn Son and his messianic mission, fulfilled in death and glorification. In Christ God calls other children to be conformed to the same image, giving them grace and evoking in them various measures of faith. Such faith engenders the renewal of their minds, the living sacrifice of their bodies, and the multiple forms taken by such "worship." It is the vast scope of this creation from beginning to end that discloses the Creator's intentionality. The "one body in Christ" is the reality that gave force to Paul's exhortations; those exhortations, in turn, are the expression not of his own genius but of the code of guidelines accepted among all the churches.

Paul grounds his authority on "the grace given to me." The same grace establishes limits to his authority, since God has given grace also to Paul's readers. Along with grace, God has given each believer a measure of faith inasmuch as God is at work in each heart through the love of Christ. This conjunction of grace and faith create "one body in Christ," and that body is God's replacement for the body of sin and death in Adam. Membership in that body makes them automatically "members of one another." The gift of grace/faith qualifies each member to contribute to the other members (12:6–8).

Those contributions take the form of obedience to quite specific commands; such obedience discloses an inner bond to the "living sacrifice" and to its ultimate origin in God's grace. These axioms have become so brief and so conventional as to shrivel into vague and sentimental moralisms, substitutes for dangerous action. But rightly seen as an action produced by the new age in its struggle with the old, each axiom is, in fact, a call to battle. We will look next, all too briefly, at three of them.

"Be on fire with the spirit."   Isolated from the chain of creativity, this can be viewed as a conventional wish for warmheartedness or as a call to charismatic frenzy. However, Paul

rarely refers to the spirit of a believer without having in mind
the interaction between the human spirit and the Holy Spirit
that God's creative activity has released, the Spirit that every-
where is at war with the flesh. And in Paul's mind, the Spirit
of God was present in the creation of all things. Accordingly,
the command to be on fire with the spirit has a rich cosmic
resonance that clearly marks each new spirit-powered action
as coming from God the Creator, whose Spirit is the source of
the believer's energy.

"Obey the Lord as his slave." The usual translation "serve
the Lord" is grossly deficient; nothing is more trite than a call
to service, especially in a "service economy." The Greek word
here, *douleuein,* denotes the obedience of a slave to a master.
And the master in this case does not make easy demands on
his slaves, because the measure of the master's obedience to
God has become the measure of his slaves' obedience to him.
Every slave is known by his master, every master by his
slaves. And no slave can obey two masters. Paul introduces
himself as a slave of Jesus Christ (1:1). It is in obedience to his
master that he writes this letter in which he now calls for their
obedience as slaves to the same master. Each slave's act of
obedience thus becomes a link in the chain of God's creativity
(6:16–23).

"Rejoice in hope." Hope in Christ is the source of joy in
Christ. As in the other commands, this hope is oriented toward the promise of sharing in the glory of God (5:2), toward
the promised redemption of the body (8:23), and toward being conformed to the image of his Son (8:29). This joy is the
form taken by inexhaustible gratitude for the gift of grace.
This hope, as Leander Keck has well argued, is governed not
by what is expected to happen in the future at some final
point on a projected timeline, but on the unfolding of meanings of what had already happened through God's rescue
from the present evil age (Gal. 1:2). Hope is grounded in the

actuality of government by grace; it is a gift *from* God that releases the movement *to* God.[8] The chain of causality and creativity runs from grace to hope to joy. It is this chain that governs the one body in Christ and produces the joy.

"Therefore . . . Bless Your Persecutors" (12:14–21)

During the first two decades of Christian history, persecution was a daily reality for every Christian congregation. Paul knew all too well about such conditions in both Jerusalem and Rome. Chapter 8 specifies some of the forms of this hostility: economic distress, unrelenting prejudice, pogroms, forced flight from one town to another, stonings, arrests, executions. The comparison to sheep being led to slaughter is all too apt. It seems clear from the evidence in Paul's letters and in the book of Acts that during these two decades the chief instigators of violence were leaders of Israel, priests, scribes, interpreters of the scriptures, and rulers of the synagogue. When civil authorities were involved, it was usually because they were responsible for "law and order" and so were forced to adjudicate between these Jewish messianists and their Jewish adversaries. In this next set of commands, then, Paul concentrates on the problem of how these messianists should respond to those adversaries. Three commands were central.

"Bless those who persecute you." Verbal curses by these enemies must be met by verbal blessings, their violent actions countered by nonviolent actions. Here a recourse to Paul's two-age thinking is again necessary for comprehending the command. God's curse had initiated the old age, and God's blessing had initiated the new. The Creator's curses on the serpent, on Eve, on Adam, on the earth, had led to Cain's murder of Abel; God's blessing through Christ on all who were implicated in the murder of the Messiah had signaled the in-

ception of the new. Thus, the blessing of their enemies by Christ's followers had become a mark of their indebtedness to God and to his Son. The return of curse by blessing, a very simple but a very difficult act, discloses the power of the new age over the old. The realm that had been ruled by the vindictive law of evil for evil has here been replaced by the realm ruled by God's peace. Each blessing has become a subversive and revolutionary action that threatens the entire history of human efforts at securing justice, in which every curse justifies a curse in return. God's Messiah had been given the authority to issue this command in order to break the vicious cycle (see Matt. 5:44).

"Leave room for the wrath of God." What had sustained the so-called law of retribution in human history was the human desire for justice—an innocent recipient of injustice should have the right to claim "revenge." In this command, Paul destroys that right. In all such cases of innocent suffering, recipients of God's grace must trust in God's justice; that is, they must "give room" to divine wrath. The term *wrath* is an alternate designation for the old age. By seeking justice on their own terms, Christians in effect would deny God's sovereignty over the present evil age. More than this, by that very effort they would themselves return to the old age and become again subject to God's wrath, the curse on Adam. That was adequate reason why they should never "avenge themselves": when instead of seeking justice they trusted in God's mysterious design for transforming enemies into friends, they would give evidence of a renewed mind. To love one's enemies was, therefore, one of the basic forms of making "a living sacrifice."

"Overcome evil with good." Modern readers easily overlook the context of this command in Paul's thought-world. In that world, to respond to violence with violence is proof of inheritance from Adam of an unrenewed mind. Conversely, the

only way to break the endless chain of evil for evil is to substitute good for evil. Jesus' death and exaltation had not only broken that chain but had introduced the messianic age by revealing how God overcomes evil according to God's creative intention. The verb *to overcome* is drawn from the vocabulary of warfare; it presupposes a decisive battle between God and his primeval enemy in which a final victory is won. In deciding how to respond to persecution, then, Christians gave their testimony concerning the relative strength of the same ultimate antagonists. Paul makes it clear that the power of "the good" is to be located in very specific actions, like giving food to the hungry and drink to the thirsty. Such actions indicate not the victory of Paul over Caiaphas, but of God over Satan (16:20).

"Therefore . . . Do Not Resist the Governing Authorities" (13:1–14)

In what follows, Paul sets forth the demands made by the renewed mind on the obedience that Christians owe to the governing authorities. In any reading, this passage provides an intriguing example of the distinction between the two ages: government by divine wrath, as expressed by resistance to the authorities, versus government by divine grace, as expressed in nonresistance.

Who were the authorities that Paul had in mind? His reference to their power to levy taxes and exact tribute indicates their status as civil authorities. In Rome and its provinces, this power was closely linked to the work of the police in maintaining order and the army's role in preventing rebellion. Other New Testament records enable us to name some of the names: Claudius the emperor (Acts 18:2); Gallio the proconsul in Corinth (Acts 18:12–17); the town clerk in Ephesus (Acts 19:35–41); and the succession of judges before whom Paul defended himself—Lysias (Acts 22), Felix (Acts 24), Festus (Acts 25), and Herod Agrippa (Acts 26). For all Christians the story of Jesus provides a familiar and decisive precedent and archetype. Paul refers to that story in a letter probably composed before the letter to the Romans (1 Cor. 2:6–8). Those rulers had "crucified the Lord of glory." They had, of course, been quite unaware of the design of God "before the ages" that required such suffering. These same rulers were "doomed to perish," even though during the present age their authority must be respected. Servants of the Messiah who respected that authority were promised a share in their Lord's glory. Their obedience to authorities would be, like that of Jesus (Phil. 2:6–11), an act of obedience to God. Jesus' crucifixion had been followed by persecution of his disciples, illustrating his proverb: like master, like servant. Jewish leaders often had taken the initiative in attacking those servants, and their attacks had led to arrests by the Roman police, to hearings, torture, imprisonments, and even crucifixions. In all of the surviving accounts of Paul's own hearings before Jewish or Roman judges, he was faithful to both Jesus' teaching and his example.

Why were these commands needed in Rome? The text itself points to an answer. The order to subject themselves implies a prior desire and tendency among Roman readers *not* to submit but to resist the authorities' actions. By their actions, the authorities had become a "terror," having used power to inflict unjustified penalties on innocent victims. These victims may have attributed the unjust actions of their victimizers to an authority received not from God but from God's enemy, Satan. If that were true, civil resistance would be a duty, since it would in effect offer resistance to Satan. Thus it was necessary for Paul to repeat that the exercise of civil authority had come not from Satan but from God.

The commands were needed also because of the probable continuing tensions in Rome due to what Roman Christians had already suffered (16:3–16). Two leaders, Prisca and Aquila, had on one earlier occasion been expelled from Rome. (It is not clear whether this took place before or after they had become Christians.) These same exiles had later risked their lives for Paul when he had been in trouble with the authorities. Andronicus and Junia, other former prisoners, were now in Rome. They had had even longer terms of service as apostles than had Paul. As former prisoners, they could testify to the injustices of their treatment by Roman authorities. Probably Epaenetus knew about earlier troubles in Ephesus. Several other Romans had served with Paul in other cities and knew of his sufferings there. So Roman believers had become well acquainted with the injustices itemized in chapter 8 and knew firsthand the earlier behavior of Roman officials.

On some occasions the authorities in other cities had defended Jesus' followers against the violence of their enemies, but on other occasions they had given way to pressures from those enemies. In Ephesus, the rulers had taken prompt action to restore order and to insist that all charges must be presented to the courts in the usual way. When troubles had erupted in the Corinthian synagogue, Gallio had dismissed the charges as involving only "your own law" and had declared Paul innocent of "crime or serious villainy." When, in Jerusalem, Jews later tried to kill Paul, the police intervened to save him from death; Lysias had considered torturing Paul to secure evidence, but had then kept him in prison until he could consult with higher authority. In Pilate's treatment of Jesus—a story with which Roman believers were probably familiar—Jesus had been declared innocent but had nevertheless been turned over to his enemies for crucifixion. After Agrippa heard Paul's defense, he also declared the prisoner innocent of the charges. Festus, however, after the same hearing, wanted to turn Paul over to his enemies, but was prevented by Paul's prior appeal to the emperor. On occasion Paul had been kept in prison to protect him from the Jews, or in hope of receiving a bribe from his friends, or in an effort to placate his enemies. The policies of the authorities were quite inconsistent or, rather, consistent only with their own shifting self-interests.

By contrast, the stories of apostolic response to the civil authorities' decisions seem to show a high degree of consistency. Though innocent of the charges of breaking Roman laws, none of the apostles had resisted arrest, torture, or even execution. However, the Gospels preserved one account of an exception. In Gethsemane, when officials arrived to arrest Jesus, one of the disciples used a sword to cut off the ear of the high priest's slave, meriting the rebuke: "All who take the sword (i.e., in resisting civil authorities) will perish with the sword (in the hands of those authorities)" (Matt. 27:57–52; Mark 15:47; Luke 22:49–51; John 18:10–11). This threat of perishing with the sword is strikingly similar to Paul's use in Rom. 13:3: "the authority does not bear the sword in vain." (In John's account of the same episode [18:11], Jesus' rebuke was supported by the question: "Am I not to drink the cup that the Father has given me?" That question implies that Pilate's decision was the form in which God had given this cup to the Son.) This sole example of a disciple's resistance to the authorities is surely an exception that proves the rule. Quite apart from the reasons why different authorities gave different verdicts for or against Christian prisoners, by their unvarying acceptance of those rulings, those prisoners testified both that God had "instituted" those authorities and that their own obedience to them was an act of obedience to God.

This history of the contacts between the apostles and Roman authorities helps to clarify the meanings Paul gives in this context to the terms *good* and *evil*. The thrust of those two simple words had been set by the commands on how to respond to brutalities of persecutors in chapter 12. *Evil* referred both to the persecutors' unjust acts against innocent Christians and to the victims' resistance out of a desire for vengeance, even when justified as a protest against injustice. By contrast, *good* referred to an action by those innocent victims in which they, for example, gave food to a hungry enemy. Only such good actions gave "room" for the wrath of God by refusing to seek justice by one's own efforts. In chapter 13, Paul continues to use these two terms in the same way, as this paraphrase may show:

> Rulers are not to be feared by those who do good (i.e., who submit), but by those who do evil (i.e., who resist). Do you want to be freed from fear of the ruler? Then do good (i.e., submit) and you will gain his approval. God has chosen him as his agent in doing good to you. But if you do evil (i.e., resist) you should be afraid of him. God gave him the sword to use as his agent in administering God's wrath to everyone who does evil (i.e., resists).

If we keep in mind the situations Paul has in mind—arrests and trials by the civil authorities—we will not misinterpret this "approval" by those authorities. There is no hint of recanting one's faith or compromising one's loyalty to Christ. Nor does Paul give a blanket endorsement of all the policies of these authorities. He does not expect their approval to take the form of dismissing all charges or of being converted to faith in the gospel. Approval may have meant nothing more than a jailer's response to prisoners' good behavior, or a decision like that of Pilate in attesting Jesus' innocence, or of similar verdicts in Paul's hearings before Lysias or Agrippa.

Of ultimate importance to Paul, of course, is God's approval. Although the authority's approval is linked to that of God, the two approvals are disproportionate, God's gift of the good being ultimate and the authority's approval being significant only insofar as the authority acts as God's agent. There is a similar disproportion between the agent's use of the sword and God's wrath. In one case, the fear is proximate, in the other ultimate. This leads us to two important considerations.

"Be subject . . . because of the wrath" *(13:5).* There can be little doubt that Paul is speaking here of the wrath *of God.*

Paul uses that term wrath (*orgē*) eleven times in this letter, in six of which he clearly refers to the wrath of God (1:18; 2:5; 3:5; 9:22 (twice); 12:19). In two verses he uses an article, *"the* wrath," and readers should treat these also as pointing to God's wrath (5:9; 13:5). In three instances the noun appears without an article, but even in these cases the contexts make reference to God virtually certain (2:8; 4:15; 13:4). In the last of these, then, it is God's wrath that the authorities administer when a Christian, let us say, resists arrest. Moreover, all eleven uses are consistent with the idea that resistance is an evil act that proves one's residence in *the age of wrath;* here the human choice registers and reflects a government by fear rather than by emancipation from fear.

This reference to an age of wrath links the commands in chapter 13 to other examples of two-age thinking that we have explored. The gospel reveals here, as in chapters 1–3, that God's wrath had governed both Gentiles (1:18) and Jews (2:5–11) until Christ died for them while they were still sinners. So, too, the age of wrath had been introduced by the sin and death of Adam and had ended only in the gift of life under the government of grace (5:18–6:11). Again, God's wrath had been expressed in imprisoning both Gentiles and Jews in disobedience in order to bestow mercy on all (11:32). There is also a very strong linkage between the logic of chapter 13 and that of chapter 8. The subjection of civil authorities to God was, to Paul, an example of God's subjection of all creation to futility (government by divine wrath), in order that all creation might inherit the same promise. By their subjection to the authorities (even by accepting arrests, floggings, and martyrdoms) and by awaiting their hope with patience, the faithful demonstrated their faith in the gospel, that "all things work together for good (the same good as promised in 13:4, 5) for those who love God . . . who are called according to his purpose" (8:28). None of the civil authorities (*exousiai*) to whom they submitted and none of the penalties that they accepted (e.g., death by the sword) could separate them from God's love (8:31–39). Both chapters thus illustrate the character of the transition from old age to new, from bondage to fear to receiving "the freedom of the glory of the children of God." To resist the authorities was to declare one's bondage to wrath; to submit was to demonstrate the kind of freedom won by their Master. God had assigned to these authorities a double function as servants (though, of course, they had no inkling of this)—they were agents both of the age of wrath and of the age of grace. However, it was the servants of Christ who alone gave their witness to God's love by choosing one age rather than the other.

The demand not to resist the authorities, we should recall, is a feature of Paul's appeal "by the mercies of God" not to be conformed to the present age. Paul does not appeal "by the teaching of Jesus," although he could have done so (Matt. 5:38–48). Nor does he appeal "by the example of Jesus," although elsewhere he does so (Phil. 2:6–11). That he does not do so here does not prove his ignorance of either the commands or the behavior of his Master. Why, then, to support a seemingly impossible demand, does he appeal "by the mercies of God"? Surely because only God's mercies through the gospel can assure the power needed for salvation (1:16). Only by putting forward "the sacrifice of atonement" (3:25) can God prove divine love for those who are still sinners (5:8). To be sure, the practice of nonresistance conforms fully to the demands and behavior of Jesus. However, it was God's design for creation, in which the bondage of all was intended as a step in the liberation of all, that provided rescue from the age of wrath for those who, by means of God's mercies through the Messiah, presented their bodies as a living sacrifice. Nonresistance to unjust and cruel authorities was a miraculous testimony to the miracle of that rescue.

Thus the wrath constitutes a major negative motivation for sharing in that miracle. The second motivation is indicated by another key word. As the image of God's wrath connotes a negative motivation, this image points to a positive motivation—the age of grace.

"Be subject . . . because of conscience."   Why, then, should the believers' conscience induce them to accept unjust arrest, torture, trial, and execution, if civil authorities so demand? That term is more than a simple noun; in this context *conscience* is a shorthand term that brings into play the entire story of how their minds have been renewed. Some clues to this story may be found in other verses where the word *conscience* appears. Paul writes about certain Gentiles whose conscience was such that what the law required was written on their hearts (2:15), suggesting that in some hidden way a good conscience and a pure heart are expressions of an ultimate divine law. When Paul wants to assure readers of the absolute veracity of his statements, he speaks of them as representing the honesty of a heart that is under the control of the Holy Spirit (9:1). In another letter, Paul identifies the Christian conscience with the indwelling Christ, in that a sin against another's conscience is, in fact, a sin against Christ (1 Cor. 8:12). Conscience is inseparable from the desire to do everything for the glory of God and not for one's own advantage (1 Cor. 10:25–29). Conscience refers to the truth that actions are governed not by earthly wisdom but by the grace of God (2 Cor. 1:12). In all these contexts, Paul stresses the decisive importance of the conscience in controlling both the integrity of speech and the purity of motive. It is a bond to the new age as embodied in the self-commitment to obey one Master, in reliance on the Holy Spirit, and in gratitude for the grace of God. It is this bond to the government by grace that in 13:5 invests conscience with awesome force. As Kierkegaard writes:

> This phrase and this thought—for the sake of conscience—
> is a transformation of language, is the Archimedean point
> outside the world, and with this, when it is deep inward si-
> lence before God, the woman who weeds the garden of the
> rich man can say that she moves heaven and earth.[9]

The rest of chapter 13 traces this conscience to its origins. In verse 8, for example, conscience is defined by the recognition that the governing authorities are included within the commandment to love. The obligation to pay them whatever respect is due is based upon and transcended by the obligation to love. In chapter 12 Paul had specified love as governing all behavior toward other members of the one body and even toward enemies engaged in persecution. Now, in chapter 13, he extends that same love to cover the whole orbit of civil obligations. Authorities are now included among the *neighbors* whom Christians must love as themselves (13:8). The Pilates and the Neros are thus located within the reach of the law that Jesus bound on all of his followers; conscience is seen to be operating wherever they obey that law.

In the conclusion of the chapter Paul provides an even more dramatic location for the hidden spring of Christian conscience. Here he presents various criteria for action that had been formulated in oral tradition to apply to many pedagogical needs, now using those more general criteria to support the call for nonresistance to unjust civil authorities.

> Besides this (the unlimited obligation to love), you know
> what time it is, how it is now the moment for you to awake
> from sleep. For salvation is nearer to us now than when we
> became believers; the night is far gone, the day is near.[10] Let
> us then lay aside the works of darkness and put on the
> weapons of light. . . .

In beginning his ethical teaching, Paul had made resistance to civil authorities an act in conformity to the present age and submission to them an act of the mind renewed in accordance with the new age. Now, at the end, Paul makes such submission equivalent to awaking from sleep in recognition of the dawning of the day. His choice of this new set of narrative metaphors—sleep/awaking, darkness/light, night/day—is by no means accidental. These metaphors activate many community memories. In his teachings Jesus had restored these metaphors to common currency so that they now resonate ultimately with the stories of creation. On the first day God had commanded "Let there by light" and had divided the darkness from the light. Now Paul traces the demand that Roman readers love all their neighbors to God's creation of light "in the beginning." To awaken is to reject the works of darkness, including the act of resisting authorities. To awaken is to live in the light of the new day and to put on a new set of clothes, the *weapons* of light. This awakening releases a vast kaleidoscope of equivalent images: the renewed mind; the presentation of bodies as a living sacrifice; rejection of conformity to the present age; the love of all neighbors; awakening from sleep; the dawn of Day One; arming oneself with the weapons of light for the Day's battle with darkness; and overcoming evil with good. The image of weapons reflects the fact that there is a war on, in which victory depends on the choice of weapons.

Paul had been dealing with Christian responses to the civil authorities, but now he widens the lens to show how those responses are linked to other battle zones:

> Let us live honorably as in the day, not in reveling and drunkenness, not in debauchery and licentiousness, not in quarreling and jealousy. Instead, put on the Lord Jesus Christ, and make no provision for the flesh, to gratify its desires.

In choosing between drunkenness and sobriety, the conscience chooses its weapons. The same is true of choices in the field of sexual behavior or in defending one's rights, dignity, or social position. All such choices reflect the weapons that are "put on" in the warfare against "the desires of the flesh." There are many battle zones, of which the response to civil authorities is only one; but there is only one war, and in that war the choice of weapons determines the victory. Paul's use of these metaphors discloses his conviction that this warfare is ultimately God's warfare with the powers of darkness. Each day's battle of the conscience is a phase of that all-inclusive warfare, in which only the weapons of light can cope with God's ultimate enemy. As Kierkegaard notes in his journal, "only what one risks everything for is a matter of conscience."[11] This conviction is what sustained Paul's demand not to resist authorities. The conflict cannot be understood if it is viewed only as pitting the Christian against a Gallio or a Festus, a Pilate or a Nero. It is a conflict between the primeval darkness and the light.

This becomes clear when we consider the significance of Paul's final command to be clothed with the Lord Jesus Christ. Here he equates the weapons of light with the Messiah. This means, of course, that Christians have available the same weapons that Jesus used in his victory over the powers of darkness, but it means more. It means that in the struggles taking place within Christian hearts, they can be clothed with the Messiah, so that their action becomes the channel by which Jesus himself exercises his sovereignty, so that this day becomes his day, his victory. Such, then, is a final definition of the Christians' conscience. It is defined by loyalty to the teaching of Jesus (as in Matt. 5–7), by respect for the example of Jesus as a murdered prophet, by faith in what God has done through the obedience of the Firstborn, and by God's love at work in Christians' hearts through the Holy Spirit. This conscience bears a triple stamp: from God, through God, to God.

In sum, Paul's political ethic is only one of many areas within which Christians are obligated to celebrate the transition from one age to another in response to God's mercies. The night had been the time for works of darkness, reveling, drunkenness, debauchery, quarreling, jealousy—all forms of gratifying the desires of the flesh in conformity to the age that had been born in Adam's rebellion. The new day dawned with this waking from sleep, with the presentation of their bodies as a living sacrifice, with putting on the weapons of light, or, more simply, with putting on Jesus Christ as their new master. Their conscience is now the necessary embodiment of this new creation, of which the words *day* and *light* are code words referring to God's purposes before their disruption by Adam's sin.

This overall perspective determines the lines of the apostle's effort to mediate another bitter conflict that had risen in Rome, and elsewhere (14:1–15:13). The conflict had its roots in mutual scorn and condemnation that arose because of varying degrees of loyalty to the Mosaic laws dealing with the Sabbath and with dietary restrictions. Some Christians were convinced that all days were alike, and that they were therefore freed from any obligation to keep the Sabbath or other holy days. They did this in honor of their new Lord; that is, when they had put Christ on as God, they had begun living in the period before the creation of the Sabbath and before the Mosaic command to do no work on that day. Similarly, some lived free from all rules that distinguished kosher from unclean foods, because in the Lord God nothing is unclean in itself (14:4). In putting on Christ as the second Adam, they had begun to live again in Eden as described in Gen. 1:29f., where God declared everything to be very good and said "you shall have them for food." Priority in creation conferred priority both in salvation and in duty (13:11).

Although the apostle agreed with this understanding of the code words *day* and *light,* he was appalled at the implications that some Roman believers had drawn from that code. A climate of suspicion had spawned mutual scorn and mutual condemnation that had resulted in the ruin of some "for whom Christ died," and thus in the destruction of "the work of God." Such actions clearly guaranteed rejection before the judgment seat of God. To overcome such a misunderstanding of the new creation, Paul defines afresh what putting on Jesus as Lord really means:

> We do not live to ourselves,
>   and we do not die to ourselves.
> If we live, we live to the Lord,
>   and if we die, we die to the Lord.
> So then, whether we live or whether we die,
>   we are the Lord's.
> For to this end Christ died and lived again,
>   so that he might be Lord of both the dead and the living.
> (14:7–9)

To Paul, those three verses defined the act of dying to "ourselves" and of putting on this Messiah as God. That act established the norm which destroyed the ground for mutual condemnations and scorn, whether believers continued to observe the Mosaic commands or to ignore them.

Paul ends his appeal for harmony by calling all readers to join with one voice in the glorification of God:

> May the God of steadfastness and encouragement grant you to live in harmony with one another, in accordance with Christ Jesus, so that together you may with one voice glorify the God and Father of our Lord Jesus Christ (15:5–6).

The code words *day* and *light,* with their reference to the new creation, had not resolved the hostilities. Each faction continued to prefer pleasing itself to pleasing its neighbors. Their new Messiah had done precisely the opposite (15:3). Consequently, the only way to glorify the Father of this new Messiah was to live in harmony with one another in agreement with Jesus' example. Christ Jesus had welcomed into his body members of all factions. Thus, they too could glorify God only by welcoming all. Only by joining in this common glorification of the same God could they give final evidence of the renewal of their minds.

This, then, was the new creation that the earthquake on Golgotha produced, according to the mind and heart of Paul— a creation that, like the death on Golgotha, gave an absolute priority to the glorification of God. One of the writings of Jonathan Edwards that was securely grounded in a thorough study of the entire Bible is his essay "Concerning the End for Which God Created the World." In his search for that *end*, Edwards found a basic clue in Rom. 11:36. "God's glory is an ultimate end of creation." "All things are so wonderfully ordered for his glory, so let him have the glory of all, forevermore."[12] Paul's witness to that earthquake enables us to see "God's act in the cross as an act that recreates the world, reconciles the first Adam and Eve to God through the self-giving love of the second Adam—Christ—and frees us from our wrong decision to become wise, and makes us fools for Christ."[13]

Paul's witness, however, carries devastating implications. The glorification of God presupposes a final condemnation on all false constructions of reality: the licentious pride of the Gentile world, the judgmental self-righteousness of the Jewish world, the power and wisdom of political and educational elites, society's futile efforts to achieve justice and equality, the hypocrisies of religious establishments, the bickering among "the saved" over food, sex, and sabbaths. By introducing the age of grace, the cross had demonstrated its power over all such manifestations of Adam's legacy.

2

The Letter to the Hebrews: A New Worship

The fo is chasit, the battel is done ceis,
The presone brokin, the jevellouris fleit and flemit;
The weir is gon, confermit is the peis,
The fetteris lowsit and the dungeoun remit,
The ransoun maid, the presoneris redemit;
The feild is win, ourcumin is the fo,
Dispulit of the tresur that he yemit;
Surrexit Dominus de sepulchro.[1]

In his opening declaration the author of the letter to the Hebrews achieves a stunning architectural symmetry and a cosmic inclusiveness of perspective. Both exegetes and theologians have been impressed with the literary skill and theological depth that appear in this carefully structured summary of what is to follow. In fact, the opening sentence might well be considered the extended title of this baffling book:

> Long ago God spoke to our ancestors in many and various ways by the prophets, but in these last days he has spoken to us by a Son, whom he appointed heir of all things, through whom he also created the worlds.

In this single sentence the narrator sets the terms for the ensuing conversation with his readers (or listeners, since the initial story was first read aloud to the community). They would not comprehend this literary appeal unless they first understood God's speech through their ancestors and unless they also understood God's speech "in these last days" through the Son. Such a word spoken through the Son had created all worlds, including their own present habitat. The same word had established this Son as "heir of all things," including their own destiny. The time of their lives was now bounded by this beginning and this end; in the meantime they were being sustained by God's "powerful word," which continued to speak to them daily through the Son. The moment of transition from one voice of God to the other was identified with the moment when the Son had made "purification of sins" and had taken his place of authority in heaven (see p. 60f.). Each day the Son continued to speak to them. Such are the terms of the conversation in which this narrator addresses his listeners; these are therefore the only terms in which they could fathom his message. They must, in fact, pay "greater attention to what we have heard" as God speaks through the Son and through those who have heard him (2:1–4).

One feature in this author's language, however, can cause a miscarriage of meaning, especially to a modern audience. Although he visualizes the ultimate origin and destiny of this community in nonliturgical language, in his argument with his readers he relies on highly liturgical images, presumably because of their own linguistic heritage. Among those dominant images are the holy city, the tabernacle, the priesthood, the daily and annual sacrifices in the temple, the altar as "the place of atonement," and the blood of animal sacrifices. Because of the profusion of these images, readers may too easily infer that God's objective through the work of the Son was simply the establishment of another ecclesiastical institution and tradition, with its own clergy and liturgical and legal routines. Nothing could be further from the author's intention. In his understanding of the new speech of God, God had made all such things obsolete. Each of those earthly institutions had now been abolished by its heavenly and eternal counterpart.[2] The tabernacle in Jerusalem was made with hands, part of the created order, while the Son had brought his siblings into a house that had not been made with hands, eternal in the heavens. He had, to be sure, become a priest, but on earthhe had not been a priest at all. The altar, on which he had made a perfect sacrifice for all time, was wholly different from the altar in the temple. His sacrifice, made in his own blood, sufficed for the "purification" of all the sins since Adam. In fact, he had rejected the necessity of "sacrifices and offerings," abolishing them in God's name, in order to show the absolute priority he had given to fulfilling God's redemptive design (10:5–10). The same radical change had taken placefor all members of the new covenant: God had put divine laws into their minds and inscribed them in their hearts (8:10–13). Consequently, when one reads about temple, priesthood, or sacrifices, one must interpret them in a radically allegorical way. Each symbol drawn from the temporal, created order points beyond itself to the eternal, uncreated realm. Because the Son was obedient to the Father's eternal design, the same eternal laws were written on the hearts of his obedient siblings.

In the ninth chapter the narrator reaches a turning point in his contrast between the temporal and the eternal realms. Here he describes the annual Passover sacrifice by the high priest in the earthly sanctuary in order to stress the significance of Jesus' Passover sacrifice in the "greater and perfect tabernacle not made with hands, that is, not of this creation" (9:11). Christ Jesus had made his sacrifice on the Golgotha altar by offering himself "through the eternal Spirit." With his blood he had sprinkled the heavenly sanctuary, purifying it and securing forgiveness of sins for all members of the new covenant. By this "single offering he has perfected for all time those who are sanctified" (10:14).

In the tenth chapter the author reaches another pivotal point in his appeal to his readers. He summarizes the basis for that appeal in four compact statements: (1) Jesus has opened a new and living way for us through the curtain; (2) we now, therefore, have a great high priest over the house of God; (3) our hearts have been "sprinkled clean from an evil conscience and our bodies washed with pure water"; and (4) we therefore can enter with all confidence "the sanctuary by the blood of Jesus." Those four basics justify a powerful *therefore* (as important as the same inferential conjunction in Rom. 12:1). Therefore let us "hold fast to the confession of our hope without wavering" (10:23). Now to abandon confidence in the face of public abuse and persecution would spurn the Son of God, outrage the Spirit of grace, and profane the blood of the "sacrifice by which they were sanctified" (10:29).

To provide the strongest kind of resistance to this wavering, the narrator recounts the stories of saints, beginning with Abel and ending with Jesus, whose lives had testified that "the things not seen" had been more real than anything in the visible world. These saints recognized that all visible worlds had been "prepared by the word of God," in keeping with the Creator's primordial design (11:1–3). The author then summons out of the invisible but real world these saints as a vast cloud of witnesses who were victims of the world's violence but who, by enduring such hostility, had been "made perfect" by Jesus' joyful endurance of the cross. Now, for the readers to waver or not to waver had become the question. Their choice determined their ultimate habitat. Two possible habitats are described in detail in chapter 12, introduced by the expression "*you have come to.*" This expression was often used to speak of congregations assembled for worship or to refer to the goal of human pilgrimages, such as the Passover journey to Jerusalem. Here, however, it signifies neither a meeting for worship nor a sacred site on the earthly map but an ultimate homeland that was invisible but by no means unreal.

The ultimate choice is first described in terms of two mountains; one is identified as Zion and the other is assumed to be Sinai. Both are sites where, throughout the ages, many congregations have worshiped and toward which many pilgrims have journeyed. Both mountains symbolize a community's bonding to its deity, to God's purposes in its creation, and to the terms of a covenant that set forth its duties and destinies. These two communities are identified by the two non-human voices to which they listened (vv. 19, 26); it was these voices that awakened memories of a long past, that renewed their initial commitments, and that relocated them on the road toward ultimate goals. These voices, uttered from Sinai or Zion, sealed the covenant without which neither community could be identified or understood. To this narrator, everything depended on whether the listeners had come to Sinai or to Zion; the choice was both inescapable and decisive.

Each of these place-metaphors, of course, is much more than a simple analogy to a single location; it is a story-metaphor that recalls the continuing saga of God's dealings with the elect people. The image of Sinai calls to mind the scriptural accounts of the revelation of the law to Moses and through Moses to the entire nation: the fire, the darkness, the tempest, the gloom, the trumpet, the voice that threatened death to anyone who came too close to the mountain (Exod. 19:16–22, 20:18–21; Deut. 4:11, 12; 5:22–27). This narrator had an uncanny power to select the most dramatic and ominous details in the familiar saga. So terrifying was the threat from this mountain that those present begged the nonhuman voice not to utter another word. Such was the mountain that *could* be touched; this imagined video was a composite construct of all the things that God had made, all that had belonged to the first creation.

The narrator identifies the other mountain, Zion, as a place that *cannot* be touched, because it is a reality transcending space and time. In this case, however, he does not dwell on details about the mountain, but moves directly into a description of eight supplementary images. The initial declaration "you have come to" covers all eight (to . . . to . . . to, etc.). Each of the eight thus becomes a corollary that helps to define the others. The use of the perfect tense indicates that the arrival of these pilgrims on Zion had begun in the past but had continued into the present. Each of the supplemental figures assumes the same origin and destination; each is a story-metaphor that covers the entire swath of its remembered history from an eternal vantage point. Each of the eight images must therefore be examined carefully.

To return to the initial image, Mount Zion. A mountain was, of course, a favorite biblical symbol of the rendezvous between God and the chosen people. Serving as a point where heaven meets earth, it was a frequent site of prayer, vision, revelation, judgment, and resurrection. The author in this case may well have alluded to Isa. 28:16, in which Sion (the Hebrew form) is seen as the place of God's judgment on the scoffers who ruled God's people in Jerusalem. They had taken refuge in lies and had made a covenant with death. On Sion God destroyed the refuge and annulled the covenant. Other early writers appealed to Zech. 9:9, where Sion is that Jerusalem to which the victorious monarch will come riding humbly on the colt of a donkey. The vision of Zion in Hebrews is a twin to John's vision of the triumphant Lamb standing on Mount Zion, where unnumbered angels celebrate the redemption of the 144,000 who had inscribed on their foreheads the names of their Father and of the Lamb (Rev. 14:1f).

The City and Its Citizens

The videographer moves quickly from the vision of the mountain to the vision of the city, whose name, Jerusalem, linked it to many scriptural texts. This is the "heavenly" city, and life lived there is a gift of the life-giving God. The adjective *heavenly* is the sign of the city's reality, not unreality. It has "permanent foundations" (11:10), in contrast to all earthly cities (13:14). It is the city of peace, fulfilling God's promise of peace. On entering this city one accepts its laws, economy, politics, culture, and language—the intricate fabric of human bonds that constitutes urban life.

The celestial character of this realm, however, is underscored by the sight and sound of countless thousands of the angels celebrating a great festival. The speaker wisely leaves to the audience's imagination the earthly events that prompted this festival. Was it the birth of Jesus, as in Luke 2:8–20? Was it the sealing of the new covenant in blood, as in v. 24? Or was it the enrollment of the firstborn in heaven? Or were the angelic hymns simply the celestial counterpart of the praise of God by God's people on earth? Whatever the author's intention, the choir of angels adds *glorias* and *alleluias* to the scenario of Zion, the living God, the city, heavenly Jerusalem, to which the reader comes. This is the space *within which* the earthly community conducts its worship and pilgrimage.

From the celestial actors the narrator quickly shifts attention to the roster of human pilgrims, some of whom are described as "the assembly of the firstborn enrolled in heaven." The enrollment in heaven implies that these enrollees are as yet living on earth. The fact of their enrollment grounds their present existence on God's creative purpose before the foundation of the world. Paul describes them as "citizens of heaven" (Phil. 3:20). Luke reports that Jesus assured his disciples that their names were inscribed in heaven (Luke 10:20). The prophet John speaks of those whose names are written in the Book of Life of the Lamb that was slain (Rev. 13:8). These images of a heavenly roster are the virtual equivalent of Paul's understanding of that foreknowledge and election which assure the faithful of their ultimate glorification (Rom. 8:28–30). The narrator further identifies these worshipers as firstborn children of God; in other words, they are siblings of the first-born Son of God (1:6). The Son through whom God had made the worlds announced in the midst of the earthly assembly that God had given him these brothers and sisters (2:12–13). Their birth and destiny in the heavenly city are thus established; this linkage to the Eternal clarifies in turn the basis of their daily duties and decisions as an "assembly" of the firstborn. Their birth as children of God preceded their birth as descendants of Adam and Eve.

Having names in the heavenly roster does not, however, eliminate genuine danger. "You have come . . . to the Judge of all." This danger is no less certain, and certainly no less rigorous, than the warning from Sinai had been. In fact, the assurance of having names written in heaven reinforces the blunt warning: "The Lord disciplines those whom he loves" (12:6). Grace does not confer immunity. As firstborn children, their own fidelity would be tested by a "consuming fire" (12:29). Grace requires full accountability.

God had already judged the next group of participants in the assembly on Zion. "You have come to . . . the spirits of the righteous made perfect" (v. 23). God had approved the sacrifice of these pilgrims, for they had been made perfect. Just as the pioneer of their salvation had been made perfect through suffering, so the assembly in heaven included those who had been made perfect. Here the speaker probably includes the huge gallery of the faithful whose stories he summarizes in chapter 11, stories ranging from that of Abel to that of Jesus himself. We will not review that entire roster. The narrator himself observes that any human audience would be too bored to listen to the entire list of those who "had shut the mouth of lions, quenched raging fire, escaped the edge of the sword, won strength out of weakness" (11:33–34). The conflict between Cain and Abel serves as an archetype for all subsequent conflicts while the "shame" of Jesus serves as their final epitome and resolution (12:1–2). It was to the spirits of all these men and women that the pilgrims on earth had come. The city of the living God thus forms a community in suffering between those who have been perfected and those still to be perfected through Jesus.

In this matter two points should be stressed. First of all, the author had already announced that these martyrs would not be made perfect "apart from us" (11:40), thus indicating that the assembly in heaven includes the faithful from all the generations on earth, from first to last—the future as well as the past. The sufferings that make one generation perfect include the sufferings of the others as well. No generation can claim a priority in fulfillment; a single assembly in heaven includes them all. The second point is this: although all the martyrs of chapter 11 had lived before Jesus, they had, according to this witness, suffered "abuse *for Christ*" (11:26). He had prepared for this emphasis by introducing the firstborn Son both as the One through whom God had created the worlds and as the One appointed as heir of all things (1:2). Accordingly, the entire assembly in heaven, including the angels, look back to Christ as pioneer and look ahead to him as perfecter. These two roles are interdependent. He is thus qualified to perform the same role for every generation since Abel (13:8), transcending all human measurements of time.

The point is so important that we may be justified in making a short detour from the argument. We find in his perspective a major contribution to the debate over the character of New Testament eschatology. Is it rightly called a futurist, a realized, or an inaugurated eschatology? Hebrews 11–12 presents still a fourth option: a protological eschatology. Here future hopes are grounded in the original design of God, so that the Omega matches the Alpha. In coming to the city of the living God, pilgrims could glimpse both the beginning and the end of their journey. Or as Jonathan Edwards observes, "As he is the first efficient cause and fountain from whence all things originate, so he is the last final cause for which they were made; the final term to which they all tend in their ultimate issue."[3]

The New Covenant

The entire kaleidoscope of heavenly images reaches a climactic focus in the seventh: "You have come to . . . Jesus, the mediator of a new covenant." Readers are clearly expected to draw several inferences from this statement. This is the first human person mentioned by name among the citizens of this city. His name is bound to evoke in memory all that the readers have learned about Jesus. The significance of that story is encapsulated in the word *mediator,* a term that implies the previous status of the readers as adversaries or enemies. In this case Jesus appears as mediating their earlier alienation from "the living God," "the judge of all." He stands between the heavenly and the earthly, between the design of the Creator and the wills of all creatures. The result of the mediation was the sealing of a new covenant between these former adversaries. Among the benefits of the covenant was their new status as firstborn children of God, with names written in heaven. The adjective *new* implies the obsolescence and removal of a former covenant, which, in this context, could have been the covenant sealed at Sinai (8:8–13), the initial covenant with Adam, or possibly both. In any case, the narrator accents the newness of this covenant and the fact that his readers have come to its mediator in person, to Jesus himself, now exalted in heaven. Through him they have not only become residents in the city of God, but have also yielded to such residence an absolute priority; through Christ's blood they have obtained eternal redemption (9:12).

Even modern readers who find superterrestrial fantasies absorbing are often baffled as to how to understand the two contrasted worlds in Hebrews 12, Sinai and Zion. They can only conclude that those two worlds are not only imagined but imaginary, the products of imaginations wholly unrestrained by considerations of time or space. Their sense of unreality in these visions of the heavenly city might be diminished by reading a careful study of modern nations and nationalism by Benedict Anderson, a sociologist. In his book entitled *Imagined Communities*,[4] Anderson defines a nation as an *imagined* political community that is both limited and sovereign.

It is *imagined* "because the members of even the smallest nation will never know most of their fellow-members, meet them, or even hear of them, yet in the minds of each lives the image of their communion."[5]

The imagined community is *limited* "because even the largest of them, encompassing perhaps a billion living human beings, has finite, if elastic, boundaries, beyond which lie other nations. . . . The most messianic nationalists do not dream of a day when all the members of the human race will join their nation. . . . "[6]

The imagined nation is *sovereign* "because nations dream of being free. . . . The gage and emblem of this freedom is the sovereign state."

"Finally it is imagined as a *community* because, regardless of the actual inequality and exploitation that may prevail in each, the nation is always conceived as a deep horizontal comradeship. Ultimately it is this fraternity that makes it possible . . . for so many millions . . . not so much to kill, as willingly to die for such limited imaginings."[7]

Anderson describes how these imagined communities link together fraternity, power, and time.[8] People derive their sense of their nation's reality from the use of maps that symbolize the importance of boundaries, whether the places are populated or not; from the fact of names recorded in the census, in telephone books, and in social security numbers, names that establish kinship where none really exists; from museums, tombs, and cenotaphs to unknown soldiers that are "saturated with ghostly national imaginings"; from sacred cities and goals of pilgrimages that feed the appetite for legends and myths of imagined origins and goals. No matter how new, nations "loom out of an immemorial past . . . and glide into a "limitless future."[9] Novels, newspapers, radio broadcasts, and TV programs all feed the confidence that a single community is moving into the future with its steady, anonymous, simultaneous activity and with its illusions of independence and interdependence. The imagination feeds daily on an infinite number of proofs of the nation's identity, uniqueness, superiority, and permanence. It is, in short, "our homeland." Along the way nations *imagine* their adversaries as well, often before those adversaries come into existence; but whether fancied or real, those adversary nations enhance the cohesion of the "imagined community" that constitutes the modern nation.

Anderson's book contains much more that helps us recognize the various types of imagined communities to which we all belong. I mention his analysis here because virtually every aspect of his imagined nation has its analogy or parallel in the two *imagined* communities of Sinai and Zion. Those biblical communities are no less real, no more imaginary, than are modern nations. In fact, if the biblical understanding of the Creator and God's design is valid, the thinking expressed in Hebrews 12 might reflect a better grasp of the true "imagined communities" than the modern nation.

To return to that chapter, the sevenfold description of the city that the readers enter would seem to be complete with Jesus' mediation of this new covenant. To a casual reader the addition of an eighth description might seem to be quite anticlimactic, though obviously the narrator did not think so. In his mind this eighth must have been highly important to be given this final position. To him it gave a much sharper definition to all seven of the previous story-metaphors. "You have come to . . . the sprinkled blood that speaks a better word than the blood of Abel." (English translators have a difficult time with the original Greek; we will soon examine some of those problems.) We must ask why the Preacher chose to add this image of a sprinkled blood that speaks. What does this voice add to the other seven?

This eighth image is obviously a continuation of the seventh. One blood that speaks is the blood of Jesus, shed on Golgotha. It is the blood by which he had mediated the eternal covenant, for as has been noted earlier, it was necessary for every covenant to be sealed with blood (9:22). The newness of the covenant is thus linked to the uniqueness of this death, this sacrifice that had revealed divine grace for God's enemies, through Jesus' love for them. Only through this blood had it been possible for the mediation to succeed; by this blood Jesus had enabled the forgiven to enter the heavenly city and had established this covenant as an eternal covenant (13:20).

The Sprinkled Blood

But the eighth image also marks an advance in thought beyond the seventh, and we must ask how it does so. What new thought is added? The answer appears when we focus attention on the phrasing of this text. The New Revised Standard Version reads: "You have come to . . . the sprinkled blood." But a more accurate, though more awkward, translation would be this: "You have come to . . . the blood of a *sprinkling*." This accent on the sprinkling shifts the focus of thought from the role of Jesus as the mediator to the role of those who are sprinkled with his blood, the *you* to whom he is speaking throughout this text. These readers had already been provided with several potential analogies to this act of being sprinkled.

For example, the author had already referred to the saving power of a sprinkled blood on the occasion of the first Passover. "By faith, he (Moses) kept the Passover and the sprinkling of blood, so that the destroyer of the *firstborn* (of Egypt) would not touch the *firstborn* of Israel" (11:28; Exod. 12:21–30). Implicit in this analogy is a contrast with the new Passover when the firstborn Son of God sprinkled with his own blood the firstborn children of God. The author also furnishes a second analogy in his account of Sinai, when Moses had sanctified the people by sprinkling them with the blood of "the first covenant." Among the lessons of that covenant was the truth that "without the shedding of blood there is no forgiveness of sins" (9:18–22; Exod. 24:3–8). Here the author quite explicitly contrasts the two covenants and emphasizes the unique efficacy of Jesus' act in sprinkling them with his own blood (9:23–24). The author draws a third analogy from the scriptural instructions for the high priest in the annual celebration of the Day of Atonement. Behind the curtain in the earthly Holy of Holies stood the ark of the covenant, the mercy seat or the place of atonement (9:1–5). Into that holiest of places only the high priest could enter, and he could do that on only one day of the year. Even then he could not enter without taking with him a sacrifice in blood for his own sins and those of his people. Yet even that sacrifice could not "perfect the conscience" of the worshipers (9:6–10). Such perfection was impossible during "the present time," the first creation. That covenant was made obsolete (8:13) when the Messiah had entered once for all time into a temple "not of this creation" and had, with his own blood, "obtained eternal redemption" for all those who were sprinkled with his blood. It is his blood that purifies the conscience so that God's people can "worship the living God" (9:11–14). This is the blood with which those who have come to the heavenly Jerusalem have been sprinkled (12:24). Through this blood they have shared in a total break with all other forms of worship.

Still the best analogy, however, to the act of being sprinkled with the blood of Jesus must be found in our basic text where the author compares and contrasts the blood of Jesus to the blood of Abel (12:24). Obviously this analogy carries thought back to an event earlier even than the Day of Atonement, or the covenant sealed on Sinai, or the Exodus from Egypt. As an event in the primal story of origins, the death of Abel at the hands of his brother carries ultimate and universal overtones. Now the author focuses attention on two bloods, and the voices of those two bloods—one of Abel and the other of Jesus. Why, we must now ask, did the narrator choose such an amazing conclusion to his composite video of Mount Zion? It would seem that he did not want readers to avoid listening in depth to those two voices. What did the blood of Abel say? And why did Jesus' blood speak better? They could not listen to the voice of Abel's blood without recalling the entire story of Abel's death, a story with which they were already more familiar than are modern readers.

An initial step is to recall the curse with which God responded to the serpent's deception of Eve: "Because you have done this, cursed are you among all animals. . . . I will put enmity between you and the woman, and between *your offspring and hers*" (Gen. 3:14–15). It is as a first fulfillment of this very curse that Genesis describes the enmity between Eve's first two children. Abel was the first shepherd, who had brought God an offering of the firstborn lamb from his flock. His brother Cain, the firstborn son of Eve, had brought the first fruit of his garden. The Lord had regard for Abel's offering but none for that of Cain, who became angry and—in spite of the Lord's warning—murdered his brother. The Genesis story makes a special point of calling attention to the *voice* of Abel's blood, when God said to Cain:

> Listen! Your brother's blood is crying out to me from the earth, which has opened its mouth to receive your brother's blood from your hand. When you cultivate this earth, it will no longer yield its strength to you, and on this earth you will always be a fugitive and a wanderer. (Gen. 4:10–12, LXX, my trans.)

The blood of Abel not only spoke—it shouted to God from the earth, the good earth of Genesis 1. This shout or groaning came from the same mouth that had swallowed Abel's blood, a shout protesting the earth's desecration and expressing its revulsion against the evil done to it. God's response was to

announce a terrible curse on Cain. The earth would no longer
support him with its food. Estranged from the earth, he
would become a fugitive and a vagrant. In breaking the bond
to his brother, he had broken the bond to the earth and to its
other inhabitants. The cry of Cain resounded through the sky:
"My punishment is greater than I can bear" (4:13). In
Hebrews the voice of Abel's blood becomes the voice of God,
shouting its warning from the earth to all of Cain's successors
(12:25). Abel's sacrifice was still *speaking* (11:4); the story of
Abel was still in force, covering all the children of Eve who
had inherited the serpent's enmity. Still in force also was
God's curse on all who had inherited Cain's anger, jealousy,
violence, blood-guiltiness. The earth still shouted its warning
to potential fugitives and vagrants. So stark is the contrast between this archetype, the voice of Abel's blood, and the other
archetype, the voice of Jesus' blood!

The Voices of Blood

Modern readers are often puzzled by this kind of thinking, in which the blood of Abel and the blood of Jesus have
voices speaking in ways that link their deaths to God's life in
the heavenly Jerusalem and to all of the residents of that city,
angelic and human. What Erich Auerbach says about the linkage between Abraham's and God's sacrifices of their sons
may be applied to this linkage in Hebrews between the
deaths of Abel and of Jesus:

> a connection is established between two events which are
> linked neither temporally nor causally—a connection which
> it is impossible to establish by reason in the horizontal di-
> mension. . . . It can be established only if both occurrences
> are vertically linked to Divine Providence which alone is
> able to devise such a plan of history and supply the key to
> its understanding . . . the here and now is no longer a mere

link in an earthly chain of events; it is simultaneously something that has always been, and will be fulfilled in the future; and strictly, in the eyes of God, it is something eternal, something omnitemporal, something already consummated in the realm of fragmentary earthly events . . . earthly relations of place, time and cause had ceased to matter, as soon as a vertical connection, ascending from all that happens, converging in God, alone became significant.[10]

So alien is this way of thinking today that readers of Hebrews must make a special effort if they are to enter this world where these vertical connections between two events provide the very substance of their meaning. We can more easily enter that world if we respond to texts like this not as historians, trained to insert every successive event into a tight temporal sequence, and not as scientists, viewing everything that happens as a result of previous causes, but if we respond as worshipers, listening together for the voice of a living God, who is living precisely because, as Jonathan Edwards insists, God continually creates every moment.[11] God speaks in terms of his purposes and not ours, creating a new situation *ex nihilo* that is in line with "the end for which he created the world" (see Heb. 1:1–2:4). When he speaks through the blood of Abel and/or Jesus, his voice creates a bond between worshipers and those two witnesses that is "no longer a mere link in an earthly chain of events." But we must now return from Auerbach and Edwards to Hebrews.

The first readers of Hebrews were assured that Jesus' blood spoke better than Abel's. Why so? It spoke of a new covenant removing the curse between God and the heirs of Cain. It spoke also of the faith of all the heirs of Abel (chapter 11). It spoke of self-sacrifice, of brotherly love, of forgiveness and grace, of the bonds forged by God between Jesus and his siblings. The Greek word for better (*kreitton*) is an adverb, modifying the act of speaking. This way of speaking was better because the shedding of this blood marked the point of access between the created and the uncreated realms, the tangible and the intangible, the shaken and the unshakable. The author had used the same adverb and adjective elsewhere on many occasions: for example, to apply to the new approach to God by a better hope than had been possible through the law (7:19) or the priesthood (7:22). Because Jesus' sacrifice was of a different order, it guaranteed better promises (8:6) and assured more lasting possessions than those plundered by the persecutors (10:34; also 1:4; 6:9; 7:7; 9:22; 11:16, 35, 40). In sum, God's way of speaking through the blood of Jesus had succeeded in shaking both the earth and the heavens so that all who were sprinkled with it might leave the "passing city" and enter "the coming city" (13:14). Thus the contrast between the two bloods provided an apt rhetorical and theological climax to the eight images: Zion, the city, the living God, the angels, the assembly of the firstborn, the Judge of all, the perfected spirits of the righteous, Jesus, the new covenant, the blood of Jesus, and now, finally, those sprinkled with his blood.

An appropriate climax, yes; but the act of sprinkling was also the basis for the appeal that followed: "Beware! Don't reject *the one* who is speaking." Who is now speaking? The Greek of *"the one"* is masculine, and not the neuter of blood (*haima*) or the feminine of the voice (*phonē*). The double warning comes from the God who is "judge of all." On earth God had warned through the blood of Abel; now God warns from heaven through the blood of Jesus.

> If those did not escape who rejected the one who warned on earth (all those guilty of the blood of Abel), how much less will we escape if we ignore the One who now warns from heaven, whose voice then shook the earth but now speaks (as predicted), "Once again I will shake not only the earth but also the heaven." This *once again* means the removal of

things shaken, all created things, in order that things unshaken may remain. (12:25–28, my trans.)

There are two bloods speaking, though God is also speaking through those two bloods. Before Cain killed his brother he had rejected the warning of God (Gen. 4:7). And the heirs of Cain had joined him in rejecting the same warning from the earth. The crying out of the earth, along with the curse that followed, was, in effect, a shaking that left the heirs of Cain aliens, fugitives, refugees, without a home on the good earth of God's creation.

The "better speaking" of Jesus' blood represents God's shaking of both the earth and the heaven.[12] This interpretation may not seem cogent until we trace a chain of reasoning quite typical of the New Testament. When the rejection of his sacrifice had angered Cain against God, God warned Cain about the sin (or demon) that was lurking at his door. When Cain succumbed to that temptation, his violence linked his seduction to that of his mother and father, and through them to the lies and deceptions of the serpent. The origins of all fraternal violence can thus be traced to its cosmic source, to a power that has many aliases: the ancient serpent, the deceiver of the whole world, the devil, Satan, the primeval dragon (see Rev. 12:7–12). Such an enemy can be defeated only by a greater power which succeeds in expelling it from heaven—that is, the blood of Jesus. In Jesus' death, God shook everything in the created earth and heaven, so that God's people might enter the kingdom that cannot be shaken. This image of the unshakable kingdom thus becomes the equivalent of all the earlier images in Hebrews 12 of Mount Zion. To accept the voice from the earth of Cain's curse and to welcome the voice of Jesus' blood is to enter this unshakable kingdom, freed from the legacy of Cain. In other words, the shaking of the heavens and the earth in the blood of Jesus is the epicenter of all earthquakes.

The Essential *Wherefore*

This chain of reasoning is confirmed by the way in which the Preacher visualized the *wherefore,* the actions by which the readers could prove that they had heard the voice of God speaking through the sprinkled blood of Jesus:

> Wherefore, in receiving a kingdom that cannot be shaken, let us have (a few manuscripts read "we have") grace in order that through this grace we may with reverence and awe offer a sacrifice acceptably to God. (v. 28, my trans.)

I have translated the Greek phrase *echomen charin* by *let us have grace* rather than, as in the NRSV, by *let us give thanks.* The difference in meaning is substantial. Here the problem of translation is real. Until the Geneva Bible (1562) appeared, the English versions were content with *we have grace.* Thereafter, translators recognized that the best Greek manuscripts used the hortatory subjunctive and so adopted *let us have* grace. This solution was adopted also by the ASV of 1901. It was only in the RSV of 1946 that the change was made to *let us be grateful,*[13] which in the NRSV became *let us give thanks.* I suspect that the RSV translation was adopted on the recommendation of James Moffatt, a member of the committee. According to his commentary on Hebrews published in 1924, he had found a precise parallel to the Greek phrase in Epictetus, Discourses 1, 2, 23.[14] According to Moffatt, the inferred meaning was this: gratitude is the one acceptable form of worship, "the real sacrifice of Christians."

I have found ample reason to fault both Moffatt's translation and the resulting inference. One must first consider the meaning of the noun *charis* as used elsewhere in this document. Apart from this verse it appears in six other verses, in all of which, as in the benediction in 13:25, the reference is to the grace *of God.* It is by approaching the throne of grace to receive God's mercy that seekers find grace to satisfy their needs (4:16).

So valuable is this gift that failure to obtain God's grace brings unforgivable defilement (12:14–17). Two texts are quite decisive; one of these stresses the salvation, the other the danger, implicit in the grace of God that has been offered in the blood of Christ. "We do see Jesus, who for a little while was made lower than the angels, now crowned with glory and honor because of the suffering of death, so that *by the grace of God* he might taste death for everyone" (2:9). That expresses the same truth as expressed in 12:24, 28: the blood of Jesus speaks better than the blood of Abel. Elsewhere the Preacher describes the danger of grace to those who reject the warning of 12:25. In spurning the blood of Christ, they profane the covenant by which they have been sanctified (or sprinkled?), and such a betrayal outrages *"the Spirit of grace"* (10:29). This is the force of *charin* in 12:28: "let us have grace" . . . "let us be sprinkled" . . . "let us be graced."

A second reason for returning to the older translation stems from the variety of possible meanings of the verb *to have (echein)*. Though the basic meaning is *to have,* one finds in Hebrews a wide range of possible synonyms. The same verb can be translated *to enjoy, to have received, to possess, to hold on to, to be subject to.* As in 1 Cor. 13:1–3, 14:1, where love is something both to have received and to pursue, so in Hebrews, grace is something that can be shared only if it is first received with the sprinkling in Jesus' blood, with being included in his new covenant. God's grace must be *received* before it can be exercised. The faithful already *have grace* in the sense in which they have a high priest (7:28), from whom they receive mercy and "find grace to help in time of need" (4:14, 15). They can *have* grace in the same sense that they can *have* hope (6:18, 19), but only if they first receive the kingdom that cannot be shaken.

A third reason for preferring the older translation is the structure of the logic, as indicated by the shape of the sentence. This imperative stands midway between a participial clause and a purpose clause. Only if the imperative is obeyed can the purpose be fulfilled. The purpose is the presentation of a sacrifice that will please God and avoid God's fire. (We have already noticed here an implicit allusion to the two offerings of Abel and Cain.) The participial phrase modifies the subject of the sentence by describing what had happened to the readers: "Let us, receiving an unshakable kingdom (through listening to God's voice speaking in Jesus' blood), *lay hold on God's grace.*" When that is done, the purpose can be fulfilled and a sacrifice can be presented that is pleasing to this most awesome God. It is this logic that leads at once into chapter 13 with its illustrations of such a sacrifice (e.g., the love of brothers, etc.). So interpreted, verse 28 provides a significant pivot between the residence on Mount Zion and the following series of commands, obedience to which constitutes an acceptable sacrifice (13:13, 16, 21). This literary or rhetorical pivot is a theological pivot as well, linking the uncreated order of Zion to such earthly actions as offering hospitality to strangers. The heart that is strengthened by this grace (13:9) can fulfill all these obligations.

Casual readers may react to the appeal in verse 28 ("to offer . . . an acceptable worship") with yawns rather than with new alertness: it sounds too much like pious sentimentality or like a preacher's call for a generous contribution—surely a letdown after such impassioned rhetoric. If so, they could not be more mistaken. To see their mistake, all they need to do is recall the endless stream of enmities proceeding from Abel's murder and realize that the stream had its source in God's having had regard for Abel's offering and none for Cain's (Gen. 4:4). Ever since that tragic moment, all human history can be summarized in the problem of what kind of human worship will be acceptable to a God who is "a consuming fire." That is the problem solved by the voice of Jesus' blood, a voice which conveys a grace of God that has shaken both earth and heaven and opened to Cain and his heirs a kingdom that cannot be shaken. That grace has disclosed the kind of sacrifice that is acceptable to God, and in so doing has revealed the original design that had been lost through the seductions of the serpent. The story of the first two brothers is the story of the entire human family; that is why the *offering*, the worship, is so significant.

This *wherefore* confronts readers with a decisive transition from the gift of grace to the kind of human offering that is, unlike Cain's, acceptable and pleasing to God. To be sprinkled with the blood of the new covenant is to be bonded to the unshakable kingdom, a bond that God protects with consuming fire. This is precisely the same kind of logical transition that we noticed in Rom. 12:1 (see p. 21f.). Because this new covenant governs the heavenly city, it creates its own politics, economics, and communal morale. We may distinguish in what follows many types of worship that are pleasing to God:

the love of brother for brother (the reverse of Cain's sin)
the welcome given to strangers by their hosts (a blessing that replaces the curse on Cain)
the willingness of the unscathed to share the lot of the prisoners (accepting the possibility of shedding their own blood)
the honor accorded to the marriage bond (in recognition of God's creation of the first parents)
the reliance on God that frees the faithful from love of money and earthly security (a return to Genesis 1)
the trust of citizens of the heavenly Jerusalem in leaders who have been chosen and sealed by God's word
the freedom from legal and religious regulations that grace gives (a gift noted in 12:28)
the vocation of priests that prevents them from profiting from the offering of the people
the mutual interdependence of followers and leaders
the sharing with others of one's resources

the going to Jesus "outside the camp" in order to "bear
    the abuse he suffered"
the loyalty to a coming city that dissolves the bonds to
    an ephemeral one
the readers' response of trust in this author

These are all introduced as examples of worship acceptable to God (12:28), and all are summarized as sacrifices that
are "pleasing to God" (13:16). It is not surprising, then, that
the closing benediction accents the same motif—God work-
ing "among us" that which is "well pleasing (i.e., acceptable)
in his sight" (v. 21). Nor is it surprising that these examples of
an acceptable offering are implicitly ways of listening both to
the voice of Abel's blood and to the voice of Jesus' blood.
Readers should notice that in the description of the heavenly
city there is no temple (as also in John's prophecy, Rev. 21:22),
and that among the acceptable offerings he mentions no insti-
tutional ritual and no ecclesiastical sacrament. Churches and
their liturgies may have an important role in the ephemeral
city, but they seem to have none in "the city that is to come"
(v. 14). Why is this?

Everything depends upon the will and design of the creator! A prior question is: why did God create the world? As
we have seen, Jonathan Edwards provides a convincing answer: God created the world for God's own glory. That motif
of glory is central to the logic of Hebrews. The Son is a reflec-
tion of God's glory (1:3), and because of "the suffering of
death" he was crowned with glory (2:9). His suffering (the
blood that speaks better than the blood of Abel) became the
means by which God "brings many children to glory" (2:10).
Behind the curtain in the Holy of Holies is the mercy seat that
is overshadowed by "the cherubim of glory" (9:5; see also
Rom. 3:25; Matt. 27:51); this is the place entered by the
Crucified. The offering of "the blood of the eternal covenant"
resulted in the eternal glory (13:21). Paul Ramsey summarizes

Edwards's thought in these words: "The work of redemption was in the counsels of God before time was, and that was the original and independent end for which God created the world."[15] All this invests this question with an ultimate importance: what form of offering is pleasing to such a Creator? It is this reasoning that underscores the significance of all these actions that result from listening first to the voice of Abel's blood and then to the voice of "the sprinkled blood that speaks a better word than the blood of Abel" (v. 24). Only worship that is pleasing to this God can fulfill God's design in creating all things.[16]

The Motivation

We have now moved partway into comprehending this concluding exhortation, but we will not fully grasp its seriousness until we grasp more fully the situation that prompted the writing in the first place. What was the situation in the author's church that induced him to write? What had been happening to his readers? Here is one clue:

> after you had been enlightened, you endured a hard struggle with sufferings, sometimes being publicly exposed to abuse and persecution, and sometimes being partners with those so treated. For you had compassion for those who were in prison, and you cheerfully accepted the plundering of your possessions. (10:32–34)

Readers should ask who the people were who had inflicted such abuse and persecution and why had they been impelled to engage in such violence. The narrator does not clearly identify these adversaries or analyze the reasons for their hatred. But he does not really need to do either; his readers know those things all too well. It should be obvious to modern readers that the source of hostility is to be found among those responsible for shedding the blood of Jesus, "the

pioneer and perfecter of faith" (12:1–4). This points directly to
those religious leaders who had condemned the Messiah for
his blasphemous attacks on the law and the temple. Consider
some of the charges now being made against these leaders.
The former covenant with God had become obsolete. The efficacy of the system of temple sacrifices had ended. The work
of the priesthood and the authority of the high priest had
been superseded. Such annual festivals as the Passover and
the Day of Atonement had been replaced by the once-for-all-
time sacrifice offered by a lonely man on an unclean hill outside the city gate. Often in the history of religions, minor
changes in modes of belief and worship cause major wars to
erupt; it is not surprising in this case, where a new covenant
had been introduced through the blood of its mediator, that
the bloodletting should continue. This narrator, however,
does not rail against the sins of those enemies, and in this respect he follows the example of his Messiah. Rather he expresses belief that persecution was the form in which this
God was disciplining humankind; God's children were being
called to endure their sufferings with the same joy as their
leader (12:3–11). Even at the moment of writing, those sufferings remained acute.

> Remember those who are in prison, as though you were in
> prison with them; those who are being tortured, as though
> you yourselves were being tortured. (13:3)

The results of those sufferings were all too clear. Some believers were losing their confidence, shrinking back from danger,
and were being lost (10:35–39). It was their weak knees in facing the threat of martyrdom that produced the long appeal to
the roster of martyrs in chapter 11. It was the insidious erosion
of faith through the fear of death that evoked the portrait of
Jesus facing and accepting the shame of the cross (12:1, 2). His
victory is presented as God's judgment on their drooping
hands and weak knees (12:12), on their fatigue and fear of

death. Jesus' blood reminded them that they had not yet resisted the tempter to the point of shedding their own blood
(12:4). To put the point quite bluntly, the author wanted his
readers to accept martyrdom for the sake of the same joy that
had been set before Jesus. To do this would allow the pioneer
of their faith to become its perfecter (12:1, 2). Only thus could
they obtain the grace of God (12:15), the grace that came with
the gift of an unshakable kingdom (12:28) and signified their
enrollment in heaven (12:23).

The issue that each reader faced was whether to fear
death, thus continuing to live under the power of the devil, or
to rely on the power of One who had destroyed the devil and
who thus had freed "those who all their lives were held in
slavery to the fear of death" (2:14–18). Only the One who had
survived that test by dying could help those who were facing
the same test. The issue for the readers was to choose between
being willing to shed their blood and crucifying the Messiah
anew (6:6). By listening to the voice of the blood of Jesus, the
readers of this book could be perfected by their sufferings. He
had tasted death for everyone; that death had enabled him to
sanctify, to make holy, the resulting sacrifices of all his brothers
and sisters (2:5–13). It was through such shared sacrifices, the
sprinkling with such blood, that God had subjected the coming world to these martyrs and had brought all God's children
to share in the power and glory of "the coming world" (2:5, 9,
10). That is the world to which the readers of this letter had
come—Mount Zion, heavenly Jerusalem, the angelic festival,
the kingdom and the grace of God. Those are the offerings that
are pleasing to God, the offerings dictated by "the blood of the
eternal covenant" (13:20).

If this interpretation of Hebrews is near the mark, the kinship between the logic of this document and Paul's understanding of the two ages in Romans should be obvious, along
with Paul's concept of being baptized into the death of Jesus
and of being crucified with him. If it provides a convincing ex-

position of the linkage between the Genesis story of the first fratricide and the suffering of Jesus in Hebrews, it should make more intelligible the forthcoming analysis of the conflict in Matthew between the heirs of Abel and the heirs of Cain, a conflict that reached its final impasse on Golgotha. Moreover, there should be many other resonances between the perspective of Hebrews and the perspectives of other early Christian documents. I suggest, for example, that Hebrews 12 discloses the existential context for understanding the Gospel accounts of the Last Supper, with their emphasis on "the new covenant in my blood," as well as the enigmatic symbolism in John 6 of drinking the blood of Jesus. God's shaking of the earth and heaven, in Hebrews, is an image that is entirely at home in the wider world of early Christian language and experience. That should become even more apparent when we examine the Matthean account of the twin earthquakes, one at Jesus' death and the other at his resurrection.

Finally, in this chapter we should observe how fully this document illustrates another characteristic of biblical literature which Auerbach cited: "The Bible's claim to truth . . . is tyrannical." The world it sees is "the only real world." Each writer calls us "to fit our own life into its world, feel ourselves to be elements in its structure of universal history."[17] How different this is from the tendency of readers who, in response to each text, attempt to fit a doctrine or a command into their own previous world of thought or action.

3

The Gospel of Matthew:
A New Vocation

Who sees God's face, that is self life, must die;
What a death were it then to see God die?
It made his own Lieutenant Nature shrink,
It made his footstool crack, and the Sun wink.[1]

My first intention in this chapter was to recover, so far as possible, Matthew's reasons for using the Little Apocalypse in chapter 24. Because I immediately discovered that those reasons were linked to his understanding of the vocation of Jesus' disciples after his death, my concern has come to include a scrutiny of that linkage. Because Matthew understood apocalyptic predictions and vocational prospects in the light of Jesus' crucifixion, my ultimate objective is to listen to his account of that crucifixion as a necessary step toward comprehending the other features in the story. I will begin at the point of Jesus' arrival with his disciples in the temple (21:12) and will end with his final instructions to them (28:18–20), hoping thus to learn something of the impact of the Golgotha earthquake on both apocalyptic expectations and vocational dynamics.

Stage Setting

Every apocalypse has a specific setting in space, time, and personnel. This segment of the Evangelist's story begins with

Jesus' arrival in the temple (21:12), where he immediately challenges the authorities by driving out the merchants and by cursing the fig tree. In response they challenge him to declare his authority for such actions; this he does indirectly in a series of parables which the authorities recognize to be aimed directly at them. This series of parabolic attacks reaches a climax in chapter 23 in a scathing diatribe that identifies the authorities as the children of Cain continuing their age-long violence against the children of Abel. It is that imagined but historic struggle that triggers the apocalyptic warnings in chapter 24. (Readers should therefore never begin their study with the beginning of that chapter.)

Throughout the literary buildup of dramatic tension between these enemies, Jesus is the only actor who is named; all others are anonymous participants in the story. He stands throughout at the center of the stage, as prophet, teacher, purifier of the temple, as Messiah, and, most important, as martyr-designate. His role is more than that of an actor; in some sense, as interlocutor and director, he controls the sequence of events with a high degree of advance knowledge of what was to follow. Underlying the role of Jesus, of course, we can discern the literary craft of Matthew himself. Although he seldom intrudes into the action, he was an able editor, and not simply a teacher in the later churches. As editor he had a dramatist's instinct for selecting teachings that fit the events and events that embodied the truth of the teachings.

The entire action takes place in Jerusalem during Jesus' final trip to Judea. His entrance into the city is celebrated as an appropriate enactment of prophecy. The arrival of this "king" shakes the city (literally, a quake), with everyone asking "Who is this?" Every preacher has explored with delight the symbolic and ironic overtones of this messianic entrance of a king riding on an ass. The story of the exit from the city, in 24:1ff. and 27:32, is just as tightly packed with symbolic meanings. This city is the holy city, a fact that added great significance to every advent and departure by its king. Even more significantly, this stage is the temple, "God's house," with appropriate nuances connected with all appearances there by God's Anointed. Here the authority of Jesus' adversaries is concentrated, and it is the place toward which all the movements of Jesus had been directed from the beginning. In the debates here his adversaries try to trap him and he proves adept in doing the same to them. His words only exacerbate their rage; theirs only strengthen his determination to fulfill his assignment. Matthew makes it clear that here in the temple an irresistible force collides with an immovable object, and that Jesus knows that such a collision is the completion of his messianic mission.

The collision moves steadily toward a violent resolution during the holiest season of the year, the preparations for the Passover, when all loyal Jews commemorate Israel's ancient deliverance from bondage and anticipate a coming deliverance with the return of Elijah (the irony of 27:47, 49). Those are days when both teachings and events serve to define the meanings that would be embodied in the new covenant sealed at the Last Supper, the awesome struggle in Gethsemane, the arrest, the trial, the execution of the Messiah as blasphemer. The opposition to Jesus had been building from the outset of the Gospel. The parables and debates of chapter 22 articulate the multiple causes of such opposition, causes that center in opposing attitudes toward the law of Moses and the messiahship.

The Actors

Throughout this segment of the Gospel, the roster of actors remains constant: Jesus, the disciples, the crowds, and the opponents, usually identified as scribes and Pharisees and later on as priests and elders. All actors but Jesus are identified as groups, which indicates that group roles are more significant than individual roles and that the significance of each group is determined by its relation to Jesus (and thereby to God). Apart from fulfilling this role, nothing is said about the personnel of the groups, their daily activities, their wealth, or their inner divisions. Two individuals, both absent, are considered of key importance to all: David and Moses. All the actors share in loyalty to them, but a sharp division exists in deciding what such loyalty demands. Is it Jesus or his opponents who understand and follow the authority of David? Who are entitled to sit on Moses' throne as interpreters of his law?

The crowds play important roles, though it is easy for modern readers to misconstrue their assignment in Matthew's scenario. As editor, he leaves little doubt about their relation to Jesus. Far from being neutral or passive spectators—"extras" in stage idiom—the crowds have heard Jesus' proclamation, have accepted his message, and on his arrival in the city acclaim him as a messianic prophet.[2] They recognize him as Son of David, which immediately alienates them from the scribes and Pharisees. From the beginning Jesus' work has been oriented toward them. He has forgiven their sins, healed their sicknesses, exorcised their demons, and welcomed them as humbled recipients of God's dominion. During this Passover season their presence with him in the temple is both a result of his former ministry and a harbinger of their future roles in the church. The religious authorities are afraid of them.

Matthew's picture of the disciples is quite different. Jesus has called them as fishermen, shepherds, farmers, and stewards, and the whole of the Gospel is designed to prepare them for those tasks in the period following his death.[3] None of them has been healed, presumably because all of them have been ordained to become healers, thus extending Jesus' ministry (10:8). In the service of God's dominion, they have left homes and previous occupations to be trained for that ministry, and they are present at every turning point in his short mission and will be present until his arrest and after his vindication. Many of his teachings, including prophetic revelations, are meant for their ears alone. Everything that happens in the temple at the Passover holds special implications for their later work. Just as Herod thought that the powers of John the Baptist were at work in Jesus, so Matthew pictures the powers of Jesus continuing in the disciples.

The Enemies

The Matthean portrait of Jesus' enemies fills the canvas with surrealist colors, between the time of Jesus' entrance into the temple (21:12) and the time of his departure (24:1). The temple, of course, is their stronghold, where few dare to challenge their authority. They are therefore angered by the shouts of the children welcoming the Son of David into this sacred shrine (21:15). They refuse to recognize the authority of John the Baptist (21:17). They are the butt of Jesus' cartoon of the son who lied to his father about his readiness to work for him (21:30). Although every parable in this sequence is a fearless and scurrilous attack on the chief priests and elders of God's people, none is more incendiary than the declaration that God would welcome whores into his dominion ahead of these pious frauds (21:31). The cornerstone which, as builders, they rejected would be used to crush them (21:44). When they reject the king's invitation to the wedding banquet for his son by killing those who deliver the invitation (the later apostles), that king will destroy the murderers and burn their city (22:7). The Sadducees know "neither the scriptures nor the power of God" (22:29). The Pharisees are hopelessly confused in their expectations of a Messiah (22:43–44). In parable after parable, attack after attack, Jesus levels curses on these hypocrites and predicts for them God's fiery retribution.

Jesus accepts their vocation as interpreters of Moses; but that very acceptance makes his attack even more penetrating

(23:1–3). As teachers of the Torah they have proved to be enemies of Moses. As he does not waver in his attack on them, they waver no less in their attack on him. But as he singles out no individual culprit, it is clear that the issue is one of the group's faithfulness to their vocation under God. By the end of chapter 23 in his appeal to Jerusalem it becomes clear that it is Israel's religious leadership as a whole that has betrayed its calling. Matthew, of course, sees such betrayal as essential to the tragedy by which, in the end, the holy city would be redeemed.

Hypocrisy Defined (23:1–12)

The opening paragraph of chapter 23 fulfills a double function. It shows that, in all the action that follows, Jesus is primarily concerned about the future of the crowds and their leaders, and it makes clear how both groups can distinguish faithful from faithless interpreters of Moses. Although Jesus recognizes a hierarchy in status and authority (Father, Messiah, disciples, crowds), he turns that order of ranking upside down; in this case his ranking is in order of service, with the crowds at the top. The disciples are forbidden to claim precedence as instructors, rabbis, or fathers; the crowds are forbidden to accord them such precedence. The boundary between the two families (or, depending on the metaphor, the two societies or ages) is drawn along the line that separates pride from humility. Only humble self-sacrifice qualifies the disciples to replace the current scribes as interpreters of Moses and thus entitles them to place burdens on the shoulders of the crowds—burdens that their predecessors have refused to carry. From early in his Gospel, Matthew is concerned with the training of those disciples; now that period of training is approaching its climactic end. Matthew understands that the suffering of the Messiah will establish an inescapable norm for the suffering of the disciples, for his death reverses the universally accepted standards both of greatness and of messianic redemption.

A clear premonition of such a reversal is given in the law promulgated by this Messiah, the law that will be illustrated fully by everything that will happen thereafter to Jesus, to the disciples, to the crowds, and to their opponents:

> All who exalt themselves will be humbled.
> All who humble themselves will be exalted.

Those passives are *divine* passives: the *self*-exalted will be *God*-humbled. This law is, in fact, a prophecy that will be authenticated in the Passion of Jesus and later in the Passion of the disciples as servants of the crowds. All that follows in the Gospel, whether discourse or narrative, demonstrates the cogency of that double prophecy. The visions of cosmic catastrophes are simply highly developed metaphors that expressed the antithesis between the self-exalted and the self-humbled.

Hypocrisy Enacted (23:13–32)

At verse 13 there is a sudden shift in the scenario. Here, without explanation, the scribes and Pharisees appear on the stage. This appearance seems to be a matter of editorial convenience more than historical accuracy; the law of Jesus requires negative exemplification. However that may be, Jesus now addresses this new audience (though still in the presence of the disciples and the crowds). Seven times the Messiah pronounces the divine curse: "Woe to you. . . . " This choice of the sacred number seven suggests completeness and finality. The seven denunciations could hardly be more sweeping or more penetrating. Although the seven woes are phrased differently, they resound with an ominous rhythm: the confrontation "you," the present tense "you lock," the charge of hypocrisy, the taunt of sightless guides presuming to guide the blind, the contradiction between outer purity and inner filth, between the demand for human veneration and the reality of divine aversion. All seven woes illustrate the divine humbling of the self-exalted. The denunciations are unrelieved by any touch of gentleness, any judicial recognition of degrees of guilt, any trace of compassion. No response is given, and none is allowed.

Scholars recognize the evidence that the seven woes had circulated separately within the Christian community before Matthew's selection and arrangement of them.[4] It seems that he arranges the order of the seven in such a way as to lead to a climax in the seventh: the contrast between the long line of martyred prophets and the long line of their murderers, who in this case have prided themselves on their tomb building and grave decoration (vv. 29–31). The seven woes also lead to a summary that applies to all, a summary that conceals an overarching perspective:

> You serpents! You brood of vipers! How can you escape being sentenced to hell? (v. 33)

Here the Messiah, speaking with the authority of his Father (vv. 9–10), identifies the ultimate source of corruption in the craftiest of the wild beasts that God has made: that serpent who lied to Eve and deceived her. Because of this successful lie, God's archetypal curse has fallen on the serpent and on his entire brood:

> Because you have done this,
>   cursed are you among all animals. . . .
> I will put enmity between you and the woman,
>   and between your offspring and hers. (Gen. 3:14–15)

That primeval story illustrates the truth of the proverb: "Sin has many tools, but a lie is a handle that fits them all." It is to this primeval lie that Matthew (or Jesus) traces the deadly enmity that these opponents represent, both as serpents and as the offspring of the first liar. That ancient story discloses the invisible structural reality that comes to the surface in the temple during the Passover. The story is more than an account of one human teacher cursing rival teachers; it is a disclosure of God's continuing wrath against every repetition of this archetypal deceit. Only this can explain the ejaculation: "how can you escape being sentenced to hell?" This ejaculation can be read simply as a violent exclamation; in that case, these liars would have no chance of escaping the penalty (a similar exclamation occurs in 3:7). Or it can be read as a genuine question that invites a range of possible answers, one of which is provided by the verses that follow it. In either case, the allusion to the Genesis curse on the serpent proves that, for Matthew, the issue is not a matter of a random and isolated instance of hypocrisy but of a deeply entrenched historical and cosmic evil.

These echoes of the Genesis story become even more audible in the important announcement that follows:

> Therefore (because of your ancestry) I am sending prophets to you, along with scribes and wise men. You will kill and crucify some of them. You will flog them in your synagogues and pursue them from town to town. You will do all this to draw upon yourselves all the righteous blood that has been shed on the earth, from the blood of righteous Abel to the blood of Zechariah son of Barachiah, whom you murdered between the sanctuary and the altar. By God's authority I declare to you that all this will come upon this generation (of serpents). (23:34–36, my trans.)

The Two Generations

This manifesto of his intention proves that the preceding woes do not represent a surrender of messianic responsibility for these children of vipers. It is *to them* that Jesus will send these very messengers—presumably in order to open the way for the serpents to escape the sentence to hell. This commissioning, which Matthew describes as the final action of Jesus (28:18–20), demonstrates both his authority over his disciples and his compassion for these enemies.

Why does Jesus specify three types of delegates? The context suggests three possible answers. (1) The sending of *prophets* recalls the self-deceptions involved in the veneration of ancient prophets. The disciples will serve as successors of those who have been murdered by the "fathers" of these blind hypocrites; the disciples will become members of the generation of Abel who has come to be recognized among Christians as the first prophet. (2) The sending of *scribes* (13:52) enables the replacement of the present incumbents on the throne of Moses; these "scribes designate" will teach the crowds all the commands of Jesus (28:19) which in turn will fulfill the great command of Moses (22:37), producing a righteousness exceeding that of their predecessors (5:17–20).[5] (3) The sending of *wise men* serves as a rebuke of the fools and the blind, and exemplifies the inner purity and integrity of the self-humbled.

To Jesus, then, the current conflict is a continuation of the primeval conflict between Cain and Abel. To Matthew, this same conflict is evoked whenever Christian leaders try to fulfill their assignments. All who engage in violent attacks on Jesus' representatives automatically become responsible for the blood of all the prophets. They declare themselves to be members of the Cain generation, offspring of the archetypal serpent. "All this," promises Jesus, "will come upon this generation" (23:36). That phrase "all this" telescopes into one reality the initial conflict between the brood of vipers and the children of Eve, the conflict between the Abel and Cain generations, between the prophets and their murderers, between Jesus and his enemies, to be described in chapters 26–27, and finally between the apostles and the synagogues in Matthew's day (24:9–14).

This comprehensive perspective motivates the final appeal that Jesus makes to the leaders of Israel before his death:

> Jerusalem, Jerusalem, the city that kills the prophets and stones those who are sent to it! How often have I desired to gather your children together as a hen gathers her brood under her wings, and you were not willing! See, your house is left to you desolate! (vv. 37–38)

Here the editor gives the text a sudden and unexpected turn in both mood and form, changing the shouted curses into a grief-stricken lament. The contrast could hardly be greater. The vitriolic charge, "the prophets whom you will murder," gives way to a hen clucking for her chicks. The God who cursed the city becomes the lover who mourns over it. Whenever God has dispatched his messengers, from Abel to Christ, the result has been his own wrath *and* sorrow. The grieving elegy proves the Creator's continuing love for this brood of vipers.

We should sense all this whenever we read Jesus' final word to his enemies: "You will not see me again until you say, 'Blessed is the one who comes in the name of the Lord'" (v. 39). To whom does that *you* refer, if not to the generation of vipers, the successors to Cain as murderers of the prophets? To whom does the *me* refer, if not to the long-expected Messiah of Israel, making his last visit to the city where he will be killed? "You hypocrites will not see your messiah again *until*. . . ." That *until* looks ahead to a time when those same victimizers will say, "Blessed is the one who comes. . . ." In this context, the one who comes will be one of the prophets, scribes, or wise men whom Jesus will send. Those who will say *blessed* to this messenger will join the crowds who have welcomed Jesus to the city with precisely the same beatitude (21:9). ". . in the name of the Lord," *Lord* now referring to either the God who wept over this city or to the Messiah who died for it. So, to summarize: when Jerusalem finally blesses the prophets sent by Jesus in the name of God, they will see Jesus again and receive his blessing. The self-humbled city will at last be God-exalted, a genuine fulfillment of messianic vocation.

That occasion will bring to a conclusion many earlier episodes in the Gospel: the trial in the wilderness, the Palm Sunday entrance, the cleansing of the temple, the cursing of the fig tree, and the series of parables aimed at the adversaries (the disobedient son, the murderous tenants, and those who spurned the invitations to the wedding feast). Both the parables and the actions of Jesus are weapons used with precision in a battle that takes place in a specific moment in the history of the city's relation to its God. In that momentous deadlock, Jesus declares God's wrath with grim seriousness, albeit with the sadness of rejected love. If there is anything more terrifying than those curses on self-deceived murderers, it is the persistent love for them embodied in their willing victim.

The Passion Story of the Disciples

We can now, at long last, take up the apocalyptic extravaganzas of chapters 24 and 25. This careful preparation has been necessary if we are to grasp their initial intent in describing the continuation of the messianic mission after Jesus' death.

In these two chapters, with very few exceptions, the words are those of Jesus addressed exclusively and in private to these messengers whom he has trained as replacements for the scribes and Pharisees. Following their exit from the temple, this final sermon on the mount (of Olives) is given in full view of the temple, the city, and the Garden of Gethsemane, where Jesus will soon meet the enemy at close quarters. Jesus takes this last opportunity to alert these messengers to the hazards of their coming assignment. The character of those hazards has been annotated in awesome detail in the previous verses: they will be flogged in their revered places of worship, hounded from one town to the next, arrested, tortured, stoned, crucified. As they take up his mission, his Passion will be continued in theirs. Accordingly, this final training session brings to a conclusion the instructions that he began on the first mountain (5:1–7:29). But because the crisis is nearer, the hazards are described in greater detail and with a wider swath of citations from scripture, ancient prophecies of doom and dawn. The opening verses not only conclude the previous chapter but give clues to all that will follow:

> As Jesus came out of the temple and was going away, his disciples came to point out to him the buildings of the temple. Then he asked them, "You see all these, do you not? Truly, I tell you, not one stone will be left upon another; all will be thrown down." (vv. 1–2)

This exit of God's Messiah from God's house is a symbolic event of the first order. It solemnly ratifies the previous declaration: "You will not see me again. . . ." It announces God's judgment, for the prediction of the temple demolition was a verbal curse on the Cain generation, uttered with full divine authority: "Truly, I tell you. . . ."

Matthew probably has a second reason for stressing that curse. Why have the disciples called Jesus' attention to these massive and ancient buildings? Surely because their assignments will evoke violent hostility from this temple, and because those buildings represent the supreme religious authority in Israel, along with its permanence and power. To counter their incipient fears and despair Jesus promises the total demolition of these imposing structures. The same words are both curse and promise. As a curse they are similar to the prediction in 23:38 of a house left desolate. As a promise, they assure the disciples that, by inheriting the same enemies, they will win a victory like his own (27:51). The conjunction of curse and promise is strikingly similar to the story of the fig tree, in which a messianic curse is immediately followed by this promise:

> Truly, I tell you, if you have faith and do not doubt, not only will you do what has been done to the fig tree, but even if you

say to this mountain, 'Be lifted up and thrown into the sea,' it
will be done. (21:21)

In one sense, of course, both curse and promise are at once
shown to be wrong. Jesus' words about the temple serve as a
major charge against him, leading to his death (26:61). Nothing
could be more persuasive than a crucifixion to prove the weakness of the victims and the power of their judges. In this case,
too, the event that disproves the curse on the temple disproves
the promise, for the authority of Caiaphas remains undimin-
ished, as Matthew well knew it would. How, then, does
Matthew expect his readers to understand Jesus' curse and
promise? One answer is given by what happens at the very moment of Jesus' death—the destruction of the temple curtain.
The temple is God's house where divine glory dwells; therefore, when God's holiness is withdrawn from it, the buildings
cease to be a temple (see p. 104).

In this language world, then, words are coded to carry
double meanings. Conventional earthly prose is used to convey prophetic visions of heavenly actualities. What is obviously untrue in one dimension reveals the truth in the other.
The curse exemplifies the law that the self-exalted will be
God-humbled; the promise reveals the parallel truth that the
self-humbled will be God-exalted. When readers decipher the
code-language used in the apocalypse, they are on the way to
a deeper understanding of it.

Signs of the End (24:3–14)

The opening paragraph of the apocalypse focuses on a
question posed by the disciples: "What will be the sign of
your coming and of the end of the age?" That question is a
staple concern in many apocalypses, and readers of Matthew
are inclined to take it at face value. But the question is one of
many in the Gospels that are designed to show a gross failure

to understand Jesus; such questions often are emphasized because they reflect misunderstandings on the part of the later readers as well as of the original disciples. As usually stated, the question expresses several assumptions: that God has set a date for the end of the age, that the date can be known in advance, that before that day dawns there will be warning signs, and that those who are tipped off can better survive the transitional turmoil. In his reply, Jesus at first appears to grant the legitimacy of the question. That is perhaps why he mentions a number of traditional signs: wars between nation and nation, kingdom and kingdom; earthquakes and famines. Such events always evoke widespread fears, and history is full enough of them to justify such fears in almost every decade. But in his later answers to the disciples Jesus proceeds to attack the disciples' assumptions, one after another, and to warn them against sharing such fears. He commands them not to be alarmed by such ominous phenomena. They must not accept messianic claimants, even those who claim his authority. "The end is not yet!" His chief anxiety is that they will be deceived. Deceived by whom? By the alarmists spawned by each successive crisis? By their own self-interest? By the devil? By all of the above? We do not know. But it is clear that Matthew appeals to Jesus to discourage all messianic excitements that are produced by emergencies of that order.

Then, as always, susceptibility to such excitement was popular among persecuted minorities, and it was this vulnerability that concerns Matthew. Jesus again repeats his announcement of the violent persecution that awaits his messengers (v. 9). He anticipates the time when some disciples will respond to the dangers by surrendering their commission. Some, like Judas, will become informers, saving their own lives by betraying the other disciples to the police. Such betrayals will infect the entire group with suspicion and hatred. Others will become false prophets by urging others to join them in less-seditious tactics. The results among the "crowds" of believers will be disastrous: "the love of the many will grow cold" (v. 12). For Jesus, however, such signs of "the increase of lawlessness" must *not* be accepted as signs of the end. In fact, he uses that term *end* in a very different way, not as the world's end but as work's end, for each emissary would be saved by enduring to the end. For him, the true end is the completion of his assignment, the vindication of his faithfulness. So, too, the other end, about which the disciples ask, will not come until *after* the disciples have given their witness to all nations. Thus the Son of Man links his return to the completion of their assignment and not to visible historical events. Such promises on his part offer genuine immunization against the apocalyptic fevers so endemic among persecuted groups that are primarily interested in their own survival.

The Desolation of the Temple (24:15–28)

The next set of predictions has always posed uncertainties for readers, and it is not strange that interpreters have been baffled. The key issue is how to understand the prediction in Daniel (9:27) of the "desolating sacrilege standing in the holy place." It has become the practice to identify this imaginary figure with some extraterrestrial evil power in some distant future that by an unprecedented act of desecration would signify the near end of the age, and thus provide an answer to the disciples' question in verse 3.

We should perhaps begin by noticing the conditions in Daniel's day that had prompted his vision: a profanation of the temple when its rulers forsook their holy covenant and seduced worshipers to join them; a great suffering among "the elect" who were plundered, taken captive, and even killed (Dan. 11:31, 33; 12:11). It should be obvious that these conditions in Daniel's days are congruent with the conditions predicted by Jesus for "the elect." It is clear that Jesus links those coming sufferings to the conflicts between the Abel and Cain generations ever since the foundation of the world. And it is also clear that Jesus has just declared that God's house *has* already been profaned and will be left desolate (the *desolate* of 23:28 and the *desolating* of 24:15 use the same root word). That text helps to identify the desolating sacrilege standing in the holy temple to be none other than the high priest, who will declare this Messiah to be a blasphemer, who will preside over the council that decrees his death, and who will, after that death, order the imprisonment of some apostles and the death of others. It is this same "sacrilege" in the temple who authorizes the Pharisee Saul to hunt down Christians who have fled from Jerusalem to Damascus and to bring them back to Jerusalem in chains (Acts 9:1, 14, 21). In fact, Matthew seems to believe that such a flight is in fulfillment of Jesus' own instructions. With the concentration of antimessianic power in God's house, these refugees have obeyed his commands. It is clear that when Jesus is killed, his disciples flee to Galilee, and that when Stephen is stoned, the other deacons scatter into various provinces. Some are executed, and those who remain in Jerusalem meet behind locked doors "for fear of the Jews."

Although this remains a hypothetical interpretation of the passage, it at least explains the desecration of the temple and the subsequent behavior of "the elect." On hearing Daniel read in church, Christians could see in Caiaphas' actions and in the dispersion of Christian prophets the fulfillment of Daniel's warnings. And that could have induced among them a vast upsurge of apocalyptic enthusiasm, in which their dangers support alarmist omens of visionaries. But not Jesus! His blunt command forbids any such resort to those alarmist leaders. *All* messianic claims must be rejected. His messengers must never be deceived by signs and wonders, whether they appear in the wilderness or in clandestine meetings. To trust such signs would be to trust in lies, for, without the slightest advance warning, the lightning will strike and vultures will begin to feed on carrion (vv. 27–28). The prolongation of his Passion to include theirs does not disprove God's love. Their mission will not fail. Deliverance will depend not on deciphering advance signs but on faithfulness and endurance. "See, I have told you beforehand" (v. 25).

War in Heaven (24:29–35)

The next prediction deals with the divine judgment that will come after that lightning bolt, after those vultures, and after the persecution ordered by the desolating sacrilege. In other words, this appeal to earlier prophecies does not provide advance warnings that diminishes the need for endurance. Cosmic symbols are now introduced, but the meanings of these symbols have already been set in the coded language of scripture, as we will see.

> The sun will be darkened
> and the moon will not give its light;
> the stars will fall from heaven,
> and the powers of heaven will be shaken. (v. 29)

In Isaiah 13 this idiom had been used in an oracle against Babylon, assuring that city of its coming destruction by the Almighty. A shaking earth, a quaking heaven, and a darkened sun bespoke "the wrath of the Lord"; Babylon would join Sodom in the final desolation (v. 19). Thus God would put an end to the pride of the arrogant (see Matt. 23:12). In Ezekiel 32 a similar code had been used in an oracle against Egypt, a lament in which the cosmic upheaval produced the desolation of the earth. The release of vultures over carrion, together with national disgrace inflicted by the armies of Babylon, signaled God's punishment of proud and self-exalted hearts. In Joel 2 the same heavenly disasters had conveyed a sharp warning to Zion itself. Before this eclipse the land had been like the

Garden of Eden; afterward, it became a desolate wilderness (v. 2). So the heavenly portents reminded Zion of the loss of paradise and of the coming day of the Messiah. Joel used the vision, of course, not to feed public panic but to evoke the rending of hearts and a return to the Lord.

It is this rich language of symbols that Jesus taps in his final instructions to his disciples. The darkened heavens connote various things: that God has revealed his judgment on a creation that since Eden has been polluted by human violence, and that this judgment is prelude to steps that God will take in renewing creation to fulfill his initial designs. One more motif in this language is conveyed by the line "the powers of heaven will be shaken." Here the heavens are seen as a battleground between God and God's invisible adversaries, a conflict begun in a primeval rebellion initiated by the lying serpent, by the fallen angels, or by Leviathan. The shaking of the powers in heaven signifies God's victory over this primeval foe that enables a corresponding victory by the elect on earth. Since this earthly warfare had taken the form of persecution of the messianic community by the "desolating sacrilege," this heavenly sign is the source of new courage and hope on the part of the elect.

The Matthean prophecy conveys that very message:

> and the powers of heaven will be shaken. Then the sign of the Son of Man will appear in heaven, and then all the tribes of earth will mourn, and they will see the Son of Man coming on the clouds of heaven with power and great glory. And he will send out his angels with a loud trumpet call, and they will gather his elect from the four winds, from one end of heaven to the other. (vv. 29–31)

Because evil has established its throne in heaven, this quake has dislodged it. That defeat has been accomplished by the Son of Man, potentially in the first temptation (4:1–11) and actually in the last. His victory has produced mourning among all the tribes of earth because it has vindicated his power and glory. Accordingly, he now exercises his authority to gather his elect in this reunion in heaven. Matthew thus uses these words of a triumphant martyr to elicit loyalty among his martyrs-designate. Readers should note, however, that everything in this segment of the vision takes place in heaven and not on earth. It is in heaven that the sign of the Son of Man appears, that his power and glory are revealed, that the earthly tribes mourn, and that the sound of the trumpet calls the elect to their reunion with him. Faith in this victory in heaven is essential to the elect on earth: "When you see all these things, you know that he is near" (v. 33).

The *you* in that assurance refers not to later futurologists but to the apostles being addressed in private on the Mount of Olives, in the shadow of the cross. *"All these things"* includes the entire sermon: their own persecution as described in 23:34–36, the actions of the desolating sacrilege in the temple, the sign of the Son of Man in heaven, and his victory over the powers of evil. When he signs this promise with the magisterial "Truly, I tell you," he establishes a firm bond between their future sufferings on earth and his gathering of the elect in heaven. And all these things are promised before that very generation of martyrs would pass away (v. 34).

We conclude, then, that this so-called apocalypse "warns against apocalyptic movements among the followers of Jesus . . . . The actual danger of apocalyptic speculation is within the church and results from a misunderstanding of Jesus as the Christ."[6]

The Apocalyptic Parables (24:36–25:46)

This interpretation of the vision is supported, I believe, by the six parables that immediately follow. Addressed by the same speaker to the same audience, they serve to underscore the requirements intrinsic to their mission. These parables are unlike many other parables in the Gospels. For one thing, they come at a very significant moment in the private instructions to a limited group. For another, they focus upon the specific duties of those disciples during the time of maximum danger from the opposing authorities. They clarify the points of convergence between their obedience to these instructions and the Messiah's gathering of the elect in heaven. And by doing that, and by following so closely the apocalyptic visions, they correct potential misinterpretations of those visions. This fact should become clear in a brief examination.

The first two parables (24:36–44) seem to fuse into one since they have the same point, although the analogy of the Noachian flood is quite unrelated to the analogy of a nighttime thief. Four times within nine verses, the apostles are warned that they will have *no* advance warning of the coming tests of their faithfulness. They must remain constantly on the alert, like the watchfulness of Jesus in Gethsemane and unlike their own sleepiness. The direst of penalties from this master are promised should they fail to keep watch. As a key to the interpretation of the apocalyptic visions, these parables show that those visions should never be used to provide advance warnings of the day or even the hour, or to express the vindictive hatred of martyrs for their murderers.

The third parable (24:45–51) tells how such alertness will be rewarded by the coming Son of Man. These messengers will be in the position of slaves assigned to the feeding of other slaves. Their master will return suddenly and unexpectedly; in fact any dereliction in duties guarantees that he will come when least expected. He will bless the faithful and wise slaves and increase their responsibilities; he will curse the faithless and the foolish, assigning them to the company of hypocrites—a somber reminder of the curses on the former scribes and Pharisees. Again Matthew uses the messianic signature, "Truly, I tell you." Matthew defines the duties of these slaves in a way reminiscent of the collaboration of Jesus and his disciples when they fed the crowds in the wilderness, and in a way to anticipate the bread and wine that Jesus will give them at the Last Supper. That food clearly symbolizes the link between serving food to others and voluntarily dying for them.

The fourth parable (25:1–13), with its image of the bridegroom and his wedding feast, continues the emphasis upon a sudden arrival in the middle of the night. The bridesmaids' readiness for that coming indicates their foolishness or wisdom. The wise are rewarded by inclusion in the long-awaited banquet; the foolish are excluded. The whole of chapter 23 provides definitions of this wisdom and this foolishness. Again, the Messiah signs this parable "Truly, I tell you."

The fifth parable (25:14–30) replaces the bridegroom with an investor of funds. This parable removes in part the ambiguity of the fourth parable, which had not specified by what kind of actions the foolish bridesmaids could have prepared themselves for the midnight celebration. The slaves of this investing master, if they are to prove worthy of his trust, must use his funds to produce income for him. Those who produce such a profit will be given increased responsibility; those who do not will be cast into outer darkness (that total loss suffered by all hypocrites). Taking this parable out of this context, readers can define trustworthiness in a thousand different ways. But in this context, the master is Jesus, who has made these men his slaves in a very definite way and has invested a very definite kind of capital in them. The whole Gospel is devoted to clarifying their duties. The character of those duties removes any ambiguity about how these slaves are obligated to reinvest his "funds."

The sixth parable (25:31–46) fulfills a triple function in this final "practitioner's guide" for the apostles. First, it serves as a climax to the series of parables. Second, it thus becomes a valuable guide to understanding the earlier apocalypse. And third, it is an effective introduction to the messianic Passion. Matthew stresses a highly elaborate introduction: the Son of

Man appears as both king and shepherd, the commander of the angels, and the judge of all nations. The climactic character of the parable is underscored by the announcement that this curse has been prepared for the devil and his messengers, and that this blessing has been the Father's design from the foundation of the world. The judgment scene is located in heaven, where the final struggle is being waged between the Son of Man with his messengers and the devil with his messengers; that very struggle has been going on from the first clash in Genesis 3 and 4.

In these two chapters, the parabolic images of the Son of Man have been various: he appears as a thief, a bridegroom, a returning householder, an absentee investor, a shepherd, a monarch—all these are traditional parabolic and apocalyptic images in Jewish prophecy. But the actions that are judged—actions that reflect that judgment scene in heaven—are the very specific duties assigned to the leaders of a persecuted messianic community on earth. Some of these duties seem to be routine and ordinary, like staffing the soup kitchen; some are long-term, like investing capital funds; and some are characteristic of dangerous emergencies. In this final parable those duties include giving food and drink to those whose goods have been plundered, providing lodging for refugees who are fleeing from other towns, caring for and visiting helpless prisoners who are awaiting trial or execution—precisely the conditions anticipated in 23:34–36. The ones providing help are the apostles; those receiving aid are brothers and sisters of the Messiah. (The NRSV translates *adelphoi* as members of my family.) They are now the *least* members of Jesus' family, in part because they are the most helpless and expendable. Apostles who minister to the Messiah incognito are fulfilling the commands that he had issued before he identified himself with them in his Passion.

Accordingly, this judgment scene marks the boundary between heaven and earth. It identifies the moment of transition between the two creations, when God makes all things new. The moment when apostles fulfill these duties is the moment of fulfillment of the apocalyptic visions: when the danger is greatest from the desolating sacrilege, when the sun is darkened and stars fall from heaven, and when these individual appointees of Jesus inherit either the curse levied on the devil or the blessing prepared for them from the foundation of the world. In this vision-parable Matthew gave his final verbal reply to the disciples' question concerning signs of Jesus' coming and of the end of the age. This answer demonstrates the folly of raising such a question. This answer also illustrates the basic law that Jesus applies both to the scribes-incumbent and to the scribes-designate: the self-exalted are God-humbled; the self-humbled are God-exalted. Such an answer is the only answer consonant with the Passion of this Son of Man, for which this parable serves as a symbolic prelude.

Clarification

As we have noted, this final parable serves to clarify the messianic confusions conveyed by the disciples' questions in chapter 24. But the clarification does not stop at this point; the most decisive clarifications take place in the events that follow. In reading these final chapters, readers should be aware of an intricate web of associations between the earlier teachings and these later revelations. The predictions of chapter 24 and the parables of chapter 25 prepared the first readers to detect meanings inherent in the Passion, while those climactic events, in turn, enacted truths that had been hidden in the predictions and parables. This interaction of messianic words and deeds discloses the presence of God's kingdom, which, as the final parable stresses, God had prepared from the foundation of the world.

From the events that follow I have selected three actions that show how Matthew understood both predictions and parables. The first of these takes place during the Passover supper, a celebration that resonates with communal memories and anticipations. At the close of the meal, Jesus

> took a cup, and after giving thanks he gave it to them, saying, "Drink from it, all of you; for this is my blood of the new covenant, which is poured out for many for the forgiveness of sins. I tell you, I will never again drink of the fruit of the vine until that day when I drink it new with you in my Father's kingdom." (26:27–29)

When this story is repeated today, congregations rarely ask what Matthew himself understood by this story. To understand his reasons for telling it, we need to place it within the sequence of earlier and later chapters, noting especially his repetition of the key symbols.

One of those is the cup. This symbol has last appeared in a discussion between Jesus and two disciples in the presence of their solicitous mother (20:20–23). She has requested exalted seats for her sons in the coming kingdom. In reply, Jesus uses a rebuke ("You do not know what you are asking") and then a test of discipleship ("Are you able to drink the *cup* that I am about to drink?"). Matthew's contemporary readers were easily able to grasp the point of both the rebuke and the test. The disciples did not know that status in the kingdom depended on "becoming last of all" and, in spite of (or because of) their self-assurance, they were not yet able to pass the test. The *cup,* as defined by his own fate, was the act of voluntary vicarious dying. Although James and John did not yet know it, drinking that same cup would be the unexpected result of their later discipleship (Acts 12:2). The same symbol appears later on, in the evening following the supper, in the prayer of Jesus to his Father: "let this cup pass from me" (26:39). These three uses of the same symbol tie these moments together in a single moment of truth. The cup which they drank at the supper was the cup that they were not yet able to drink, yet it was also the cup that they would drink new with him in the Father's kingdom. These three cup-texts are subtly interrelated. As a covenant in Christ's blood (26:28), the cup conveyed a forgiveness of their earlier sins of self-confidence and self-deception (20:28). His acceptance of the cup in Gethsemane (26:42) enabled them later to join him in self-sacrifice and in God's kingdom. Thus defined, the cup covenant showed how foolish had been their questions about the end of the world (24:3) and how wise his warnings for them to stay awake (24:46).

In the account of the supper there is another key symbol, "my blood of the covenant," the meaning of which Matthew suggests in earlier and later events. Matthew has prepared his readers to understand the connotations of this term *blood* by using it as a summary of the entire history since Cain and Abel (23:29–36; see above, p. 79). Jesus has identified all of Cain's heirs as those who shed the blood of the prophets. The antithesis is the blood of the heirs of Abel, including not only Jesus himself but also those prophets whom he would soon send, who would be known by their "innocent" or "righteous" blood. As we have seen, each instance of the taking and giving of blood marks for Matthew the recurrence of the serpent's successful lie in the Garden. The blood that Jesus shares with his disciples at the Passover is given for *many* in forgiveness of their *sins* by God. The earlier summary defines both *sins* and *many* in terms of the generation of Cain. Though it is like the blood of Abel (see Heb. 12:24; see p. 57f.), this blood is yet unlike it in being God's gift of forgiveness to all the murderers of Abel.

Matthew clinches this understanding of the Passover meal in his account of what happens the very next day. Then Judas confesses that he has betrayed "innocent" or "righteous" blood (27:4). Pilate emphasizes his own innocence, though readers know better than to absolve him completely. The people, in turn, accept full responsibility for Jesus' blood. In this deft way the editor again defines the *many* whose *sins* are forgiven by Jesus' Father. He also deftly defines the identity of those who drink the cup with him in the Upper Room and those who would drink it with him in the kingdom of God—that is, the disciples who are pledged to the same forgiveness, not only as recipients but also as donors of blood. In Jesus' action of sealing this covenant, then, this narrator discerns the meaning of the predictions in chapter 24 and the parables of chapter 25. To him all later celebrations of this Passover will be included within the first; in them all Jesus will pour out "my blood of the covenant" as both a gift of forgiveness and a test of discipleship.

I want now to examine a second clarifying event that happens in Gethsemane when Jesus is arrested. In his account of this incident the narrator calls special attention to the swordplay on the part of one of the disciples (26:50–56). All four Gospels show a rare consensus in reporting this incident, a clear proof of its importance, but Matthew detects in it a hidden meaning that is well worth observing. He alone introduces the account with a sharp exclamation *idou*, which I think the NRSV translators have wrongly rendered by *suddenly*. Literally this verb is a command: *look*, or *see*: it calls attention to some unusual aspect of this incident. In the nativity stories, for example, the command accompanies appearances of angels in dreams; it also punctuates the successive stages in the journey of the kings (1:20, 23; 2:1, 9, 13, 19). Thereafter, it signals the activity of heavenly potencies in the ministry of Jesus: his baptism and temptation (3:16–17; 4:11); his power over demons, leprosy, sickness, and unruly waves (8:2–34); his authorization of delegates (10:16; 28:20); his meeting with Moses and Elijah (17:3, 5); and his death and postmortem appearances (27:51; 28:2, 7, 9). This exclamation appears four times in the swordplay account, a clear warning of hidden implications, as if the editor were warning his readers: "Slow down here, look for unusual coincidences, listen for unexpected echoes." There are clues here to divine activity, to cosmic conflict, to moments of messianic power.

Matthew tells of two men, one dispatched to arrest Jesus and one of those "with Jesus." Matthew does not, like Luke or John, name them, but both men have hidden identities. The first is a slave of Caiaphas, the high priest, acting with his full authority. Jesus earlier had warned that this highest of the religious officials would seize him and turn him over to the Gentiles (16:21; 20:18). It is in the palace of Caiaphas that the Council meets when it decides to arrest Jesus by stealth and to kill him and also when they conspire with Judas (26:3–5, 14–15); it is there that they will agree on the death sentence (26:57–66). In his action Caiaphas embodies the power that from the time of Cain had murdered the prophets (23:35–36), power that would be terminated in the earthquake on the following day. Such is the power vested in the person of his slave.

In one sense, that slave is the aggressor. However, in Gethsemane Jesus orders his opponents, "Do what you are here to do." With this word Jesus refuses to defend himself; so when his disciple acts, it is in defiance of the declared will of his master. Matthew earlier has insisted on describing the disciples as slaves of Jesus (10:24–25; 20:27) and has accented the impossibility of one slave serving two masters. Jesus has carefully prepared the group for this very moment of betrayal. In his choice of symbolic language, the narrator makes it very clear that the action is indeed a betrayal.

"He stretched out his hand," thus mimicking the action of the adversaries; in biblical parlance, this action is an assertion of force and a threat of violence.[7] Again, the act of drawing his sword is another bit of mimicry, since the adversaries have come with swords and clubs. In this resort to counterforce, the disciple engages in action pathetic in its futility and culpable in its betrayal of Jesus' instructions as a bearer of peace (10:5–31). Presumably the disciple thinks he is defending Jesus; Matthew tells the story in such a way as to show the tragic contradiction. The sword slices off *the ear*. Why should this wound be significant? Surely there are more vital organs. But not in biblical imagery. Generally, the function of the ear is to hear; the function of a slave's ear is to obey. The slave's ear represents his obedience to the high priest in arresting Jesus. To cut off his ear is to sever that line of authority. Actually, Jesus' disciple, in his disobedience to his master, demonstrates his own loss of hearing. That disobedience proves that he has no understanding of the kind of war Jesus has been fighting in God's name: it is as if he has cut off his own ear.

Jesus, however, at once corrects the tragic error: "Put your sword back in its place." Then he utters the messianic law: "all who take the sword will perish by the sword." Unfortunately, that law has been taken to cover all people in all conceivable circumstances. In Matthew the focus is much narrower: it is directed at Jesus' slaves in Gethsemane, to apply to that occasion and to similar crises that they would face after his death (23:34). Here Jesus rules out the use of a sword in either his defense or their own self-defense. If they resist, the sword they use will bring against them the sword of persecution (see Rom. 13:4). That would mean the defeat of Jesus' mission, since they would be refusing to use his own chosen way of announcing God's kingdom, with its "forgiveness of sins." Any disciple who commits such an act cannot be a child of that God (5:43–48). In effect, by using a sword, the disciple is also committing suicide, in that he has ceased to be a slave of Jesus.

His action, of course, implies that the fate of Jesus and his mission depend on the outcome of a duel between this David and this Goliath. This implies, in turn, that the two causes and kingdoms are ruled by comparable kinds of power. It is to correct this delusion that Jesus refers to twelve legions of angels in his Father's army. The disparity is not only between one person and twelve legions but between wholly different kinds of power (not unlike the point of the dialogue between Jesus and Pilate in John 18:36–37). In his initial temptations, Jesus had refused to rely on the power of angels (4:6); now, in his last temptation he refuses again. At bottom, then, the disciple's sword is proof of his fear—a fear that to Jesus is like the fears of the arresting posse. His enemies had been afraid to arrest him while he was teaching in the temple. So, of all the actors on the Gethsemane stage, Jesus is the only one without fear, despite (or because of) his clearly being the most helpless!

Such courage is sustained by his understanding of scripture and of its disclosure of God's design. "The Son of Man must suffer." Why is this necessary? His acceptance of the necessity of suffering separates the Messiah from the expectations both of his disciples (v. 54) and of his enemies (v. 56). But how did Jesus come to recognize this necessity? We do not know. As a solution of this mystery, we should not so much search for an isolated verse in one of the prophets as listen to Jesus' summary of the entire span of the biblical story. The best instance of such a summary we have already examined— the perennial conflict between the descendants of Cain and descendants of Abel. Jesus believed that the current impasse was simply the climax of that archetypal struggle: "All this will come upon this generation" (23:36). That text was fulfilled in what happened. On his arrival in the holy city, the crowds had hailed him as the prophet from Galilee, but the chief priests and scribes were angered by such a welcome (21:11, 15). From that moment to the sentence of death, the conflict steadily became more intense, vindicating Jesus' awareness from the beginning of his work that he must be rejected, thus joining the line of martyrs since Abel. So, in 26:56 he places the accent on the scriptures *of the prophets,* since this is the line that he represents. In choosing individual texts, he chooses those that epitomize this whole story:

> The stone that the builders rejected
> has become the cornerstone,
> This was the Lord's doing
> and it is amazing in our eyes. (21:42)

Here Jesus traces both the rejection and the fulfillment of the architect's plan to "the Lord's doing." Such are the scriptures to which Jesus appeals in Gethsemane, scriptures that both his enemies and disciples have fulfilled without knowing it. As heirs of Cain, they have refused to bring an offering to God that God would accept; but not so, Jesus.

> Whoever wishes to be first among you
> must be your slave;
> just as the Son of Man came
> not to be served but to serve
> and to give his life a ransom for many. (20:27–28)

In that earlier declaration Jesus had recognized that messianic suffering was a necessary implication embedded in God's law of greatness. Only slaves can become conduits of God's ransoming love. Such is the law that Jesus obeyed in Gethsemane.

We may now be in a position to grasp why the narrator uses the emphatic warning, *idou,* to introduce the swordplay in Gethsemane. The two masters, Caiaphas and Jesus, are present in their two slaves. Those two masters, in turn, are heirs of Cain and Abel, encapsulating the whole history of obedience and disobedience, gentleness and violence, from the beginning. When we read the story of Gethsemane in these terms, the story yields excellent clues to the reinterpreted apocalypse of chapter 24 and to the cautionary parables of chapter 25.

The Earthquakes

Now, at long last, we come to the climactic story of what happens on Golgotha. The effort to cope with this dramatic account requires maximum flexibility in our response to Matthew's language and logic. Consider, for example, the associations of the term *earthquake* itself. This is an image that modern readers are almost bound to misconstrue. In the language of scripture, it is the powerful presence of God that shakes cities and mountains, the heavens and the earth, and whatever has been the measure of stability and security. It is God's voice that causes the earth to tremble, for that voice utters judgment and wrath—an extreme emergency designed to evoke instant consternation, terror, awe, contrition, confession. When God speaks, everything that has seemed to be permanent and reliable suddenly becomes as deceptive as "smoke and mirrors." The shaking of the foundations destroys every trace of human complacency and self-righteousness, though even in the midst of the tremors many mortals fail to perceive them. Like all evidences of the Creator's activity, an earthquake separates those who perceive a change in the balance of power from those who are quite unaware.[8]

> Darkness spread over the whole earth from noon until three o'clock in the afternoon. About three, Jesus shouted with a great voice . . . "My God, my God, why have you forsaken me?" . . . Then Jesus, having shouted again with a great voice, yielded up his spirit. (27:45–50, my trans.)

At noon begins three hours of darkness over the whole earth! Obviously, this night is not the kind of darkness that priests or thieves would notice, or did notice. Rather, it is the kind that signals such a shaking of the powers of heaven as Jesus has predicted in the apocalyptic forecast of 24:29. Such a struggle between God and those rebellious powers in heaven also resonates with the Genesis account of the initial separation of light from darkness in Gen. 1:2–4. (The darkness and light of Day One of creation were not of the same order as the darkness and light of Day Four, when God created sun and moon. The Golgotha phenomenon was of the first order.) This darkness is a symbol of the blind self-righteousness and cynical guilt of all who mocked Jesus so mercilessly, the very ones for whom he was offering atonement.

This darkness also is the measure of his dereliction, a fore-sakenness by God, and not simply his suffering from the savage mockery of everyone present. For a genuine Messiah, the fulfillment of God's will is an all-encompassing passion; to be forsaken is therefore an incommensurable loss. What darkness could be greater than such a noonday trauma?

To describe the shout by which this Messiah hurls his final question at God, Matthew twice uses the adjective *great* (*megas*). Drawn from the apocalyptic lexicon, this adjective often signals the mysterious conjunction of God's activity and human reactions. As a portent of transcendent purpose, it is often misunderstood—as is true in this case. Matthew finds this adjective most appropriate in describing the joy of the magi in finding the one born to be King (2:10) as well as the joy of the women at hearing the message of the angels at Easter dawn (28:8). Those two joys provide a well-chosen *inclusio*. Isaiah's promise that the Gentiles would see a great light (4:16) is fulfilled when the Gentile centurion sees what happened at the crucifixion, another *inclusio* (27:54ff.). Earlier, the disciples have been terrified by the great storm and amazed at the great calm (8:24–26). *Great* is the best adjective to indicate the signs of apocalyptic judgment (24:21, 24, 31; 7:27), as all other activities of the great King (5:35). Small wonder that Matthew uses it twice to describe Jesus' cry.

His timing of the cry is also very significant. It comes not at the onset of darkness but about three o'clock, when light overcomes the darkness. The cry is synchronized with the return of light, a victory that recalls the primal creation of light. This light is God's answer to the Messiah's question of "Why?" The forsakenness is intended as a declaration that God has reversed all human expectations of divine judgment and messianic deliverance, all human calculations of defeat and victory, death and life. This reversal is so great that the truth is sealed not by words but by events that reveal God's power and wisdom (see 1 Cor. 1:18–25). It is this transition from darkness to light that is registered in the tremors of the earth.[9]

The first of these tremors takes the form of ripping down the curtain of the temple, a destruction that is clearly linked to the moment of Jesus' death cry. "*At that moment* the curtain of the temple was torn in two, from top to bottom" (27:51). The translation "at that moment" renders the Greek word *idou*, a command often used for heavenly epiphanies when God acts in ways that are neither expected nor easily recognized: "See . . . Look . . . Take notice . . . Ponder!" Often it is a warning that calls attention to the danger of misjudgment: "Beware." Often it underscores an event that can too readily be ignored. In this case, the violent ripping of the curtain bespeaks God's rejection of the power and the authority of the temple to control access to God or to administer divine curses and blessings. When this Messiah pours out his atoning blood, he terminates the need for, and the justification of, temple, priests, and sacrifices. At the Place of the Skull, the priests and elders are quite unaware of this destruction. Nevertheless, the death of this Messiah constitutes God's judgment on the Pharisees of chapter 23; on the Jerusalem of 23:37; and on all who are guilty of Jesus' blood, in chapter 27. Their house is, in fact, left to them desolate (23:37). God, by shaking the heavens, destroys the barrier between his people and "the Holy of Holies," and yet at the same time declares an amnesty for all who share the sin of Adam and the murder of Abel.

> . . . and the earth was shaken, and the rocks were split, and the tombs were opened up, and many bodies of the holy ones who had died were raised, and, having come out of the tombs, after his resurrection they entered the holy city and appeared to many. (27:51–53, my trans.)

In the Greek text all of this is part of a single sentence, indicating that the death of Jesus activates all these phenomena as part of a single transformation. For instance, the same Greek verb is used to describe the ripping of the temple curtain and the splitting of the rocks. In "forsaking" Jesus, God splits open the tombs of the prophets, which had been beautified by the Pharisees (chapter 23). His death brings life to saints from many places and times, whose holiness has qualified them for residence in the holy city. As successors of Abel, they now enter the city of God. This is hardly the city that killed the prophets (23:37), but the heavenly city whose residents can now rejoice in their vindication (see Heb. 12:23). The light of the new creation penetrates tombs, which now surrender their authority over the dead. The communion with all forsaken saints is now realized through the forsakenness of this Messiah. The apocalyptic language of earthquakes has many other implications, of course, but these are some of the more obvious. By forsaking Jesus, God has terminated the authority of both the temple and the tombs. The account of God's victory over the tombs, a detail that the narrator seems to have added to the earlier tradition, inserts a subtle bit of irony into the picture. Following the emancipation of these saints from the tombs, Joseph of Arimathea, a rich disciple who owns a tomb of his own, tries to imprison in it the body of Jesus! Equally futile are the efforts of the soldiers to prevent the theft of Jesus' body from Joseph's tomb.

Another authority is present at the Place of the Skull, the authority represented by the centurion and his detachment of Roman soldiers.

> Now when the centurion and those who were with him, who were keeping guard over Jesus, saw the earthquake and what had happened, they were so terrified that they said, "Truly, this was God's Son." (27:54, my trans.)

In doing their duty, these officials represent the power of the only superstate of the time. Few countries were then willing to challenge that power. The effect of the quake is therefore apparent: it reverses the balance of power between the rulers and the ruled. The centurion testifies both to the powerlessness of government to prevent what has happened and to the intervention of a quite different kind of power. (How amazing that this confession amazes none of those present!) Simultaneously, his testimony implies that the quake eliminates the distinction between Gentiles and Jews, further evidence of the demolition of the temple curtain.

To Matthew and his readers the centurion gives his witness to the truth that God has undermined the authority of all those who have shared in the rejection of God's messenger: scribes, elders, priests, Pilate, soldiers. One mark of their rejection has been the taunts used to demonstrate the helplessness of the Messiah. Now the earthquake signals the truth denied by each of those taunts and thus destroys the credibility of all those who were so sure of their own righteousness. Any reader can test the reality of this reversal by reading each of the taunts in the light of the shaking of both the heaven and the earth.[10]

There is one inconspicuous detail in Matthew's narrative that reveals a special interest on his part. This is the presence of one of the women at the Place of the Skull: Mrs. Zebedee, the mother of two prominent disciples, now absent (27:56). Matthew had introduced her to his readers immediately after Jesus' final prediction of his Passion and immediately before the final entrance into Jerusalem (20:20 ff.). On that earlier occasion she had begun to anticipate the day of triumph when Jesus would be enthroned in his kingdom. In view of that prospect she had requested for James and John appointment to the two posts that would command the greatest power and prestige in that realm. In telling the story of Jesus' death, Matthew wants readers to recall that incident. What Jesus had then said to Mrs. Zebedee has now been fully proved: "You do not know what you are asking." Such knowledge can be communicated only when on Golgotha he receives his authority as Lord, and where only thieves are also enthroned—one on his right hand and one on his left. Now it is all too clear what it meant for her two sons to drink the cup. Matthew wants readers to discern the links between those two appearances of Mrs. Zebedee. The earthquake discloses to readers the route by which the Messiah has received his authority as Lord and the qualifications of those who would share such authority with him.

> The crown he wore was on the pointed thorn;
> In purple he was crucified, not born.
> They who contend for place and high degree
> Are not his sons, but those of Zebedee.[11]

In the earlier scene, Jesus had noted how Gentile rulers established and protected their sovereignty. In the later scene, by crucifying Jesus they illustrate that same kind of authority; but now, in their terror, they confess that God has given an entirely different kind of authority to the Son (20:25; 27:54). In the earlier scene, Jesus had disclosed to disciples that God would grant thrones in the kingdom to those who had been slaves on earth (20:26–28). Golgotha fully discloses God's verification of that truth. The expectations of the disciples are shaken no less violently than the prestige of priests, the righteousness of scribes, and the power of soldiers. By making the last first, God has made the first last. Only language that is inherently apocalyptic can do justice to such a revolution in human ways of measuring status, but, by the same disclosure, God rejects all apocalypses that covertly reinforce those human ways.

Matthew tells of two earthquakes: one on Friday, freeing the saints from their tombs, and an "aftershock" on Sunday, revealing to the women what has happened. Both resurrections mark a fulfillment of Jesus' prophecies and a defeat of death. And because his death is an atonement for the sins of many, both signal victory over Adamic sin. In becoming last of all and servant of all, a status assured by his forsakenness, he has become truly God's Anointed, sent to deliver God's people from sin and death. Although the two quakes thus fulfill similar functions in the story, other functions are entirely distinct. For example, the Friday quake, which accompanies the death-cry and the restoration of light, announces God's action of destroying the temple, with its priesthood and sacrifice, and opening the way to forgiveness of sins for all. Simultaneously, in the splitting of the rocks, it demonstrates the power to free saints from their tombs. That quake forces the centurion into his panic-stricken confession, with its many implications. Briefly stated, then, Friday's earthquake proves the validity of Jesus' announcement that all authority in heaven and on earth has been given him (28:18).

In Matthew's story, the Sunday quake plays a somewhat different role. For one thing, it provides a line of communication between the events of Friday and the missing disciples. That line is provided by the women whose presence the narrator takes pains to note, first at the execution, then at the burial, and finally at the discovery of the empty tomb. The women's role is essential to the story, as indicated first by the instructions given by the angel and then by Jesus himself. The women apparently are not aware of the Golgotha quake and its repercussions, an ignorance remedied on Sunday when they come "to see the tomb." Instead, they first see an angel; and as they run to deliver the angel's message, Jesus himself meets them with the assurance that the disciples will *see* him on the Galilee mountain. (The verbs for *seeing* are very central to this narrative, occurring no fewer than ten times in twenty verses.) Like the women, the disciples, on seeing him, worship him—a clue to his new heavenly aura. The story thus assumes that if the women had not delivered their message, the disciples would not have known that Jesus had been raised from the dead. Nor would they have known of Good Friday's investiture of the Messiah with "all authority."

Matthew's story of the work of the Messiah begins with the first victory over the devil, the opening call to repentance, and the call of the disciples with the promise to train them as fishers (4:19). It ends when the Messiah, having been invested with all authority, shares that authority with his disciples, who, in turn, can use it to bring penitents from all nations under the authority of Father, Son, and Holy Spirit. This chain of authority carries with it many consequences that the risen Lord makes very explicit. Everything that Jesus commanded before his death now carries with it the heavenly authority revealed in the two earthquakes. All the commands in the Sermon on the Mount, all the instructions in chapter 10 about the mission to the cities of Israel, all the rules in chapter 18 covering internal church discipline, and all the parables demanding watchfulness, in chapters 24 and 25—all now carried the unfathomable weight of God's authority as disclosed on Good Friday and Easter Sunday. All have been verified, and none more clearly than the law concerning self-humiliation and self-exaltation. "The kingdom of the heavens has come near. . . . Repent."

After the two earthquakes nothing can ever be the same. The return of light on Good Friday and the dawn of Easter clarify every episode in the preceding story; the presence of that light is often marked by such inconspicuous linguistic signs as "See" (*idou*), "great" (*megas*), or "Truly, I say to you" (*amēn legō humin*). The aura of mystery around many of the parables becomes more transparent. The significance of Jesus' works of mercy come to the surface, as does the meaning of former conflicts with his adversaries. To this narrator, the events themselves establish links between what has happened since the baptism by John, what happened during Jesus' Passion, and what continues to happen through the presence of the living Lord whenever followers are baptized into the Triune Name. The Father's action in forsaking and in vindicating the Son gives a redemptive dimension to everything that will happen thereafter.

This interrelatedness of the various periods in the story can be illustrated by almost any chapter in the Gospel, but it may suffice here to examine two earlier chapters (10 and 11) to show how they give a preview of Golgotha and how Golgotha reveals many of their implications. Chapter 10 serves as both an account of a "practice run" for Jesus' messengers in Galilee before Golgotha and a preview of their work afterward (28:18–20). Let me itemize some of these connections:

- With the obvious exception of Judas, the personnel of the harvesters is the same.
- Both before and after Golgotha, it is the gift of authority over unclean spirits that enables the apostles to gather the harvest.
- In both harvests they announce the approach of the kingdom of heaven by word and deed, relaying either the "peace" of life in the kingdom or the curse of joining Sodom on the day of judgment. (The Genesis blessing and curse serve as prototypes.)
- The hazards of their work are precisely the same as those accepted by Jesus and the same as he predicted for his messengers after his death. These hazards include loss of life for his sake and in his name.
- In chapter 10 as in chapter 24, the fulfillment of their assignment is correlated to the return of the Son of Man; the fearlessness with which they meet their fate becomes a measure of their understanding of the apocalyptic parables of chapters 24 and 25.
- Rewards for their service will be shared with all who welcome them, since they will be acting as surrogates of the Messiah *incognito,* as he acted as surrogate for his Father *incognito* (10:40–42).

- Baptism in the Triune Name will be fulfilled when, in their interrogation before the authorities, their sacrifice "in my name" will also represent the voice of the Father speaking through the Spirit (10:20–22).

Other observations might be made, but these will illustrate how the pre-Passion stories in chapter 10 prepare readers for the post-Passion harvesting, and how the earthquake on Golgotha discloses unsuspected dimensions in these prior preparations.

In similar fashion, the stories in chapter 11 prepare readers to understand the final scenes in the Gospel. The whole of this chapter presents a triple answer to a question propounded by emissaries from John the Baptist: "Are you the one who is to come?" From the very beginning of his narrative Matthew has been engaged in answering this question: Jesus is the Messiah! (1:1). Now his triple answer both summarizes Jesus' work in Galilee and anticipates the later collisions in Jerusalem.

First, the initial and most direct answer to John's query is given immediately (vv. 4–14). This answer points first to the more visible responses to Jesus' work: "what you see and hear." Then it points to John's own work as Elijah, completing God's intentions through the entire succession of prophets. No one born of women (i.e., no descendant of Eve) is greater than John. This implies that all heirs of the kingdom, as firstborn children of God, are greater than the descendants of Eve. To these two appraisals of his own ministry and that of John, Jesus appends two warnings. "Let anyone with ears listen!"—implying that hearing ears are rare. "Blessed is anyone who takes no offense at me"—implying that many would indeed take such offense. These warnings are ominous premonitions of the end of the story, when at Golgotha no one can hear and all are offended (with the possible exception of the women from Galilee).

The second answer to John's question takes the form of specifying how already in Galilee many have been offended. The cities have refused to respond either to John's call for mourning or to Jesus' call for rejoicing. Yet in offending these cities, both John and Jesus vindicate their credentials (vv. 16–19). Chorazin, Bethsaida, and Capernaum have refused to humble themselves, claiming rather to be "exalted to heaven." Because the deeds of power have been greater in them than in Sodom, God's judgment on them will be even more severe (also 10:15). This rejection by the Galilean cities is as much a part of the answer to John as the contrary evidence of good news to the poor (11:5), and as the later rejection in Jerusalem by the chief priests and scribes.

The third answer to John (vv. 25–30) begins with Jesus' prayer in which he thanks his Father for both the negative and positive results of his message. The God of the heavens and the earth had hidden "these things" from the self-confident and proud cities and had disclosed them to the humiliated and helpless, the nobodies, and the know-nothings. Both the curse and the blessing of God are signs of God's gracious will, God's plan from the foundation of the world, even now being disclosed to the poor in spirit. This prayer in Galilee reminds Matthew's readers of the prayer in Gethsemane and of the cry on the cross, all three prayers exerting paradigmatic significance for the apostles in their own later Passion stories.

This third answer to John's question continues in two verses in which Jesus makes four key assertions, the first of which is "All things have been handed over to me by my Father." This appears to give an unambiguous answer, "Yes, I am the one who is to come. God has given me authority over all things." Jesus has been exercising such authority in his exorcism of demons and in his preaching good news to the poor. His blessing of the poor and his curse on the self-exalted have, in fact, represented God's own judgment. This transfer of authority, however, cannot be understood apart from the second assertion: "No one knows the Son except the Father." The truth of this assertion is demonstrated when Peter, at Caesarea Philippi, responding to a question from Jesus, declares "You are the Messiah, the Son of the living God" (16:6). Jesus, in turn, announces that his identity as Son had been revealed to Peter by "my Father in heaven." This revelation becomes the rock on which Jesus would build his *ecclesia*. (In the parallel image in Heb. 12:23, this is "the *ecclesia* of the firstborn who are enrolled in heaven.") Matthew's readers are assured that the Gates of Hades will never destroy that *ecclesia*. (In Hebrews the *ecclesia* of the firstborn receives a kingdom that cannot be shaken.) Caesarea marks the verbal disclosure of God's identification of Jesus as the Son; Golgotha discloses, by way of the earthquake, the actual identification. At the very moment when no human being knows the Son, God acknowledges him.

In Matthew 11 Jesus also says: "No one knows the Father except the Son." Here again, Caesarea gives an illustration in the words of Jesus. As the Messiah, he knows that the Father's plan requires of him as the Son that he "undergo great suffering . . . and be killed" (16:21). Peter's rejection of such a requirement proves that he does not as yet know the Father; instead he knows only the mind of Satan, which prevents him from knowing "the things of God." Again Golgotha enacts the truth. No one who is there can conceive of a heavenly Father who would require that his Son die; the taunts prove as much. Only the earthquake conveys such knowledge.

In Matthew 11, Jesus makes a final assertion: "No one knows the Father except . . . anyone to whom the Son chooses to reveal him." Caesarea Philippi discloses the nature of that exception. The Son, who would suffer, could reveal his Father only to those who would "take up their cross and follow me" (16:24). The reality of that exception is proved when the disciples flee from Gethsemane and when no one at the crucifixion "knows the Father." Such knowledge Jesus shares with the eleven at their rendezvous on the Galilean mountain 28:16–20).

It is precisely such knowledge that enables Jesus to issue his invitation, in chapter 11. The logic underlying that invitation may become clear if we change the order of the clauses.

> I am gentle and humble in heart.

The story of Jesus makes gentleness and authority synonymous and also makes humility and divinity synonymous. Gentleness/authority and humility/divinity provide a clear and simple definition of all the titles and images Matthew uses for Jesus: King, Messiah, Lord, Shepherd, Son of Man, Son of God. All four attributes are illustrated in the initial temptation in the wilderness, in the work of teaching and healing, and supremely in the humility/humiliation on Golgotha:

> [Therefore] my yoke is easy, and my burden is light.

What constitutes the yoke is not made clear: the yoke of discipleship? Of the covenant? Of living by God's plan? This context suggests that it is the yoke of his gentleness, whether to friends or to foes. What constitutes the burden? This context suggests that the burden is his humility.[12]

> (Therefore) come to me, all you who are weary and are carrying heavy burdens, and I will give you rest.

It is the forsakenness of Jesus on Golgotha that gives authority to this invitation. In becoming last of all and servant of all, he can give rest from all the burdens that exhaust those who are trying to become first, the burdens carried by the proud and self-willed.

> [Therefore] take my yoke [gentleness?] upon you and learn from me [my humility?], and you will find rest for your souls.

Coming at the end of the triple answer to John's question and in anticipation of the scene at Golgotha, this invitation is issued as an expression of Jesus' authority as Son and of his intention to fulfill his Father's plan.

It may be that in this invitation to those wearied from carrying heavy burdens Jesus alludes to Sir. 40:1–11, in which the heavy yoke of hard work has been laid on the children of Adam as a penalty for their rebellion. In that case, Jesus, in promising rest for their souls, is speaking of a new age of grace which God has opened to the humbled in heart. It is the crucified Savior who calls "Come to me. . . . "

In the whole of chapter 11, then, Matthew arranges successive episodes in such a way as to uncover many layers in Jesus' answer to the question, "Are you the one who is to come?" These are some of the implied answers: "Yes, but my messiahship is inseparable from my gentleness and humility. Yes, but no one knows this but my Father. Yes, but this humility hides not only who the Son is, but, more importantly, who the Father is. Yes, but gentleness/authority and humility/divinity alienate and judge the cities, even while they give sight to the blind, cleanse lepers, and raise the dead. Who has ears that can hear such a word? Who will take no offense at me? Who will accept my invitation? Those who do so, will know who the Son is."

Significantly, the same question is raised at the final examination, when the high priest orders, "Tell us if you are the Messiah, the Son of God." The Roman governor asks, "Are you the King of the Jews?" Here the answers are given not so much by words as by deed. Jesus answers both questions by his gentleness, his humility, his forsakenness, his shame. God answers by shaking the earth. That double answer provides the warrant for Jesus' farewell to his messengers:

See! (*idou*) I am with you through all the days until the end of the age.

The best background for understanding this promise is the biblical tendency to treat as synonymous God's promises (1) to be with the chosen people and (2) not to forsake them (Deut. 31:6, 8, 17–18; Josh. 1:5; 1 Kings 6:13; 1 Chron. 28:20; Ps. 38:21; Heb. 13:5). Because of Jesus' own forsakenness on the cross (27:46), he can guarantee the fulfillment of this promise. We may also discern here a final clue to the interpretation of the apocalypse of chapter 24. Because the risen Christ will be with them until the consummation of the age, they can ignore the frantic warnings of impending catastrophes. Fears of imminent chaos can be overcome as long as he is with them, and that will be as long as they obey his commands. Because of his authority he will be with them from the inception of their mission to its end, when the only question he will put to them will be "Who then is the faithful and wise servant?," to which the answer will be "the one whom his master will find at work . . . " (24:45–46). This promise replaces apocalyptic frenzy with vocational discipline.

We have noticed that throughout Matthew's narrative he has frequently reported Jesus' announcement that the Son of Man must suffer and be crucified. Gethsemane and Golgotha have proved the accuracy of that prediction. We may now notice that just as frequently Jesus has coupled the announcement of his own destiny with the declaration that all who would be his disciples must take up the cross and follow him. Those predictions have not yet been fulfilled, at least within the pages of the Gospel. But Matthew does not allow his story to end before Jesus repeats that requirement, before he shares his authority with them, and before he promises to be with them until the successful completion of their own mission. The forsaken one will not forsake them so long as they carry the cross. His final promise thus fulfills the promise with which Matthew begins the good news: "They shall name him

Emmanuel, which means 'God is with us' " (1:23). His own forsakenness ensures that presence. Such an earthquake discloses an ultimate shaking of the powers of heaven.

In a letter of Paul to Corinth we may discover another witness both to the restoration of light at Golgotha and to the final promise of Jesus on the Galilean mountain.

> We do not proclaim ourselves; we proclaim Jesus Christ as Lord and ourselves as your slaves for Jesus' sake. For it is the God who said "Let light shine out of darkness" who has shone in our hearts to give the light of the knowledge of the glory of God in the face of Jesus Christ. . . . We are afflicted in every way, but not crushed; perplexed but not driven to despair; persecuted, but not forsaken. (2 Cor. 4:5–9)

A contemporary poet has confessed that the ancient story of Golgotha can still evoke both terror and confidence.

The Elbowed Tree

I am delved by a love
That deep son of God caught
In a hover of death
From Jehovah's red dove
When fire untied the knot
Of water, burnt Christ's breath
Coming up from the river
To sword and to saviour.

And I will not, huddled in
The bones of my pleasure
Forget the stride of his word
Through the limp of my leisure,
Nor his hands' comfort
On my bruises of sin.
Only he terrors me
Because his gospel bells

Me to my golgotha,
When my multitude hunger
Sighs fishes and bread.
From the elbowed tree
His long darkness reaches
Me hope nailed to danger,
While traitor within my head
A green cock screeches.[13]

Epilogue

> He saved others; he cannot save
> himself. He is the King of Israel; let
> him come down from the cross now,
> and we will believe him. He trusts in
> God; let God deliver him now, if he
> wants to; for he said, "I am God's
> Son."
> —Matthew 27:42–43

Some readers, now that they have persevered to the end, will ask for the point of the story as a whole. Although I welcome their perseverance and grant the legitimacy of their desire, I resist any such summary. It may be that the three witnesses *are* the point in themselves. To attempt to separate the point from the stories would require distilling a doctrine of the death of Jesus that would enable us then to discard the stories. Rather, their witness is such as to impel readers to visualize themselves somewhere within the stories which, as we have observed, have no end within the pages of the three documents. Matthew, for example, so tells the Golgotha story as to raise questions in his readers such as: Who other than God recognized Jesus as his Son? Who other than this Son recognized God as his Father? On what terms did Jesus share that knowledge with others? Why was that knowledge shared with the infants who ac-

119

cepted the invitation from this humiliated Lord and denied to the wise and the powerful? And how did this double reception become an occasion for gratitude on the Son's part? There is no single point that can do justice to a story with so many implications.

To tell the truth, in preparing this manuscript, I have not wished to convince readers of any thesis regarding these witnesses. Rather my effort has been expended in questioning the witnesses. I have wanted for my own sake to penetrate the inner world of their thinking, with its retrospect and prospect, a retrospect that includes all that they had learned about Jesus and a prospect that includes the dangers and difficulties they faced in their effort to fulfill their vocation under Jesus. Because my concern in this volume has been to listen to their words, when my readers have problems raised by those words, my inclination is to ask how those witnesses would react. Let me illustrate by examining three perspectives that inhibit understanding.

First, modern readers often discount the merit of these witnesses by observing that "all things continue as they were from the beginning of creation" (2 Pet. 3:4). Because, by accepted definitions of messiahship, a Messiah must change the human condition for the better, the obvious truth that all things "continue as they were" disproves the messiahship of Jesus. What comes into play here is precisely the same logic as that of Jesus' enemies at Golgotha. Matthew fully recognizes the force of that logic. According to his text, those enemies were entirely unaware of the earthquake; it produced no change visible to them. Even the centurion's amazing confession seems to have amazed no one but him. Unchanged were the shame and impotence of the messianic claimant, as well as the righteousness and power of his adversaries. Moreover, in the months following, Jesus' messengers had to face the same fate from the same adversaries; for them, too, nothing had changed in this respect. Yet they continued to give their witness that, with God's identification of Jesus as his Son, everything had changed. Subjectively, they knew this because their fears had turned into faith. Objectively, they knew it because God's Son in his suffering had disclosed to them God's design from the foundation of the world. God had revealed his glory, which as a Christian poet later notes, "is least like what men agree to praise."[1] Has there been no change? I think these witnesses would continue to refer to the earthquake and to do so without hesitation or qualification. Contrary evidence would be for them as old as the self-assurance of Caiaphas and even as old as the serpent's temptation of Eve.

Second, other moderns cannot accept this conviction of the ancient witnesses for almost the opposite reason: that is, too many changes have rendered the Scriptures obsolete. These highly sophisticated thinkers are overwhelmed by evidence for the vast expansion of the universe, far beyond the reach of ancient imaginations. One must, of course, give full weight to the explorations of macrocosmic interstellar space and accompanying efforts to explain the origins of the universe. One must also reckon with the penetration into the microcosmic worlds of quarks, atoms, cells, and human genes. Inquiry focused within and beyond the self has stretched human thoughts to cover ranges of reality unknown to ancient thinkers. Were messiahship to be measured by observable change, there would be many messianic claimants today. The power to change both inner and outer environments has been so great as to elicit disdain for anyone so foolish as to point to what happened on a lonely hill so far away and so long ago. Contemporary sciences have fostered a culture of disbelief that leaves no room whatever for faith in Jesus as the Messiah of God.

How would Paul respond to this outlook? Would he feel that his argument, in Romans, has been completely outdated? I think not, because I believe that he would insist that there are no fewer lords and gods in our day than in his. I believe he would find as much conflict among these gods as ever. Have sin and death ceased to be structural elements in the human self and the human society? Have scientists ceased to be men and women, with desires similar to those of Adam and Eve? Does no one today inherit the legacy of Cain? Have all the signs of futility and captivity disappeared from creation, thus eliminating the need for a hope that is based on something more permanent than the latest computer model? I, for one, think that what Paul says about Jew and Gentile in Romans 1–3 he would find applicable to all readers—premodern, modern, or postmodern. He assumed that Psalm 139 articulates a dialogue that all persons engage in with their gods. And he believed that, as Son of God, Jesus decisively changed the course of that dialogue.

Third, an even more searching series of questions has been raised by the tragedies that have recently erupted in all parts of the earth. Their magnitude is so great that they seem to dwarf all previous experiences of injustice, including that of Jesus on the cross. How can the suffering of one man long ago atone for the murder of six million human beings in Hitler's death camps? How can the first Good Friday be compared to August 6, 1945, when in Hiroshima a single bomb incinerated more than a hundred thousand innocent civilians?[2] Can the Golgotha earthquake throw any light on the quakes that have desolated the Sudan, Ethiopia, Angola, Vietnam, Nicaragua, El Salvador, Guatemala, Cambodia, Mozambique, Liberia, Afghanistan, Azerbaijan, Somalia, Rwanda, and Bosnia? Whether we look at recent history through a microscope or through a telescope, the view makes us hesitate to claim redemption through the suffering of an ancient prophet in Judea.

How, then, would our three witnesses speak to these current worlds of agony and despair? I have no doubt that they would be even more sensitive than most of us to the range and depth of human suffering. Such sensitivity was part of their burden of cross-bearing. Also I have little doubt that they would continue to speak of the distinctiveness of Jesus' suffering. He volunteered in a vocation that entailed total self-sacrifice from beginning to end. He viewed that vocation as obedience to his Father's design and as a manifestation of that Father's love for his enemies, with forgiveness of their sins against him. The shame and humiliation of Jesus' death reveal God's presence in that very forsakenness, thus qualifying Jesus to invite others to share in burdens made lighter by that presence. Jesus' weakness released a power that shook the heavens and the earth, with results that Matthew's story of Golgotha makes clear. The letter to the Hebrews visualizes that same shaking as God's voice speaking through the blood of Jesus, sealing a covenant that enabled others to enter the holy city. Paul sees in that same sacrifice God's offer of grace and peace to all the children of Adam. All three witnesses testify to the truth that the Golgotha sacrifice is distinctive in its power to represent all suffering. By referring to the blood of Abel, both the letter to the Hebrews and the Gospel of Matthew represent all of Cain's successors who rely on violence and bloodshed. By referring to the death of Adam, Paul represents all who have sinned or will sin through their trust in the serpent's lie. The death of Jesus is fully representative of Everyone's fear of death; it thereby frees them from that fear (Heb. 2). Golgotha is most representative of all, perhaps, in that it discloses the character of the warfare in heaven between the source of truth and the source of lies, between the Creator and the rulers of darkness, who are ultimately the source of the frustration and futility of creation. It is this all-inclusive scenario that makes the good news of Golgotha so distinctive and so representative.

These considerations may entitle us to venture answers to the question as to how the three witnesses might respond to the vast sufferings in all twentieth-century tragedies. They might well respond by referring to the same imagined war in heaven between God and Satan. By referring to imagined ways in which defeats and victories on earth disclose the power of those heavenly antagonists. By referring to imagined ways by which the story of Cain and Abel is a transcript of all fraternal violence and the story of Adam and Eve a transcript of the struggles that take place in every human heart.[3] By referring to signs of the old age and the wrath of God disclosed therein, and to signs of the new age where the blind begin to see and captives go free. I believe that, in remembering the earthquake, these witnesses would find signs of both ages among Jews in Buchenwald and Buddhists in Hiroshima, where hearts overcame the fear of death and the hatred of enemies, and where—in many private Gethsemanes—decisions were made comparable to the decisions of Jesus. Contemplating the worst conceivable disasters, I can even hear Paul saying again, "God imprisoned all in disobedience so that he may be merciful to all" (Rom. 11:32).

In earlier pages (see p. 53f.) we called attention to Benedict Anderson's definition of nations as "imagined communities," suggesting that religious communities can be defined in the same way. This sociologist is convinced that all communities that are larger than primordial villages are in fact imagined, and that they should be judged not by whether they are false or genuine but by "the style in which they are imagined."[4] He believes that the great religious communities have survived in part because of their profound awareness of the depths of human suffering. By comparison he finds those communities deficient that are imagined by "evolutionary/ progressive styles of thought."[5] If they recognize at all the whole range of contemporary agonies, they do so in an "impatient silence." Whether that judgment is just or unjust, I am convinced that the three witnesses to whom we have listened would find in such episodes as the Holocaust and Hiroshima a confirmation of the realism of the gospel and evidence of the continuing presence of their imagined city of the living God. If "there is a balm in Gilead" (Jer. 8:22) for victims and survivors of Holocausts and Hiroshima, it may be found, according to the invitation of the three authors, in the God who was present on Golgotha and whose voice continues to shake the heavens and the earth.

Notes

Prologue

1. Richard Roberts, *That Strange Man upon His Cross* (New York: Abingdon Press, 1934), 123.

1. The Letter to the Romans: A New Creation

1. F. W. Faber, *Pilgrim Hymnal* (Boston: The Pilgrim Press, 1962), 369.

2. L. E. Keck, "Paul as Thinker," *Interpretation* 47 (1993): 27–38.

3. H. K. McArthur, "Christology in the Predicates of the Johannine *Ego Eimi* Sayings," in *Christology in Dialogue*, ed. R. F. Berkey and S. A. Edwards (Cleveland: The Pilgrim Press, 1993), 135.

4. Keck, 30.

5. J. D. G. Dunn, "Pauline Christology: Shaping the Fundamental Structures," in *Christology in Dialogue*, ed. Berkey and Edwards, 99.

6. K. Cragg, "The Singer and the Song: Christology in the Context of World Religions," in *Christology in Dialogue*, ed. Berkey and Edwards, 187.

7. P. S. Minear, *Christians and the New Creation* (Louisville: Westminster John Knox Press, 1994), chapter 3.

8. Keck, 29.

9. S. Kierkegaard, *Journals and Papers*, tr. H. V. Hong and E. M. Hong (Bloomington: Indiana University Press, 1967), 1:683.

10. S. Kierkegaard, *Christian Discourses,* tr. Walter Lowrie (New York: Oxford University Press, 1940), 221–27.

11. Kierkegaard, *Journals and Papers,* 1:321.

12. J. Edwards, *Ethical Writings,* ed. Paul Ramsey (New Haven, Ct.: Yale University Press, 1989), 467, 475–76.

13. A. R. Brown, "Perceptions and Transformation in Paul's Preaching," in *Ecumenical People, Programs, Papers* (Collegeville, Minn.: Ecumenical Institute, 1993), 14.

2. The Letter to the Hebrews: A New Worship

1. William Dunbar, "On the Resurrection of Christ," in *The New Oxford Book of Christian Verse,* ed. D. Davie (New York: Oxford University Press, 1988), 22.

2. S. Lehne, *The New Covenant in Hebrews* (Sheffield, U.K.: Academic Press, 1990), 50.

3. Edwards, *Ethical Writings,* 6.

4. B. Anderson, *Imagined Communities* (New York: Verso, 1991).

5. Ibid., 6.

6. Ibid., 7.

7. Ibid.

8. Ibid., chapters 8–10.

9. Ibid., chapters 9–11.

10. E. Auerbach, *Mimesis* (New York: Doubleday Anchor Books, 1957), 64–65.

11. Edwards, *Ethical Writings,* 35.

12. P. S. Minear, *Christian Hope and the Second Coming* (Philadelphia: Westminster Press, 1954), 163–74.

13. L. A. Weigle, *The New Testament Octapla* (New York: Nelson and Sons), 1284–85.

14. J. Moffatt, *The Epistle to the Hebrews* (New York: Scribner's, 1924), 222.

15. Edwards, *Ethical Writings,* 532, n. 1.

16. My interpretation of 12:25–28 in the previous pages is quite different from that found in most commentaries and the ground for it may not be obvious. It is based on two convictions: first, that the two voices in vv. 25–28 are the voices of the two bloods in v. 24; and second, that to understand what God is saying through the two voices we

must recall simultaneously the Genesis story of Cain's murder of Abel and the Gospel stories of Jesus' death. When we do that, we uncover the following clues:

- There are *two* voices in v. 24 and *two* warnings in v. 25.
- The same Greek verb for speaking is used in those two verses.
- The warning God gave on earth may refer to his warning of Cain in Gen. 4:7.
- The refusal to hear that warning led to the curse on Cain and all his descendants.
- The shaking of the earth in v. 26 may refer to the revulsions of the earth on drinking the blood of Abel in Gen. 4.
- The warning from heaven in v. 25 is the voice of Jesus speaking through his blood to believers after his exaltation to heaven.
- The contrast between the uncreated and the created orders in v. 27 corresponds to the better speaking of the blood of Jesus.
- The acceptable worship in v. 28 resonates with both the unacceptable offering of Cain and the acceptable offering of Abel in Gen. 4.
- The significance of *brotherly* love as the first definition of an acceptable offering recalls the character of Cain's sin.
- The stress on hospitality to strangers recalls the character of the curse on Cain as a fugitive and homeless wanderer.
- The call to respect the marriage bond reminds readers of the story of the bonding in creation.
- The call to go outside the camp and the city in 13:12–14 may recall Cain's call to Abel to go into the field.
- The voice of Jesus' blood may be heard in the gift of the kingdom in v. 28 and in the grace that enables the faithful to make an acceptable offering.
- The blood of the great shepherd in 13:20 recalls the blood of Abel, the first shepherd.

17. Auerbach, *Mimesis*, 12–13.

3. The Gospel of Matthew: A New Vocation

1. John Donne, "Good Friday, 1613," *The New Oxford Book of Christian Verse,* ed. D. Davie (New York: Oxford University Press, 1988), 68.

2. P. S. Minear, "The Disciples and the Crowds in the Gospel of Matthew," in *Gospel Studies in Honor of S. E. Johnson, Anglican Theological Review* (March 1974): 28–44.

3. M. J. Wilkins, *The Concept of Disciple in Matthew's Gospel* (Leiden, Netherlands: E. J. Brill, 1988), 126–72.

4. P. S. Minear, "False Prophecy and Hypocrisy in the Gospel of Matthew," in *Neues Testament und Kirche,* ed. J. Blank and J. Gnilka (Freiburg, Germany: Herder and Herder, 1974), 76–93.

5. D. E. Orton, *The Understanding Scribe* (Sheffield: Academic Press, 1989), 153–68.

6. D. Patte, *The Gospel According to Matthew* (Philadelphia: Fortress Press, 1987), 336.

7. D. Senior, *The Passion Narrative According to Matthew* (Leuven, Belgium: Leuven University Press, 1975), 129–30.

8. For typical samples of this image, see Ps. 18:1–15, 60:2; Isa. 64:1–3; Jer. 4:23–28, 10:10; Ezek. 12:17–20; Joel 2:10; Sir. 16:17–23; 2 Esd. 16:8–17.

9. P. S. Minear, "The Messiah Forsaken . . . Why?" *Horizons in Biblical Theology,* forthcoming.

10. D. B. Howell, "Matthew's Inclusive Story," *Journal for the Study of the New Testament,* suppl. ser. 42 (Sheffield: JSOT Press, 1990), 239–42.

11. John Dryden, "The Character of a Good Parson," *The New Oxford Book of Christian Verse,* ed. D. Davie (New York: Oxford University Press, 1988), 133.

12. In his far-reaching contrast between Christian and non-Christian literature, Erich Auerbach finds that Matt. 11:25 is often cited in Christian texts, where humiliation and exaltation are deeper and higher than in non-Christian texts and where they belong together. Sublimity and humility are combined "in overwhelming measure, especially in Christ's Passion," 15, 132ff.

13. Arnold Kenseth, *The Ritual Year* (Amherst: Massachusetts Writers and Artists Press, 1993), 116. Used with the author's permission. Italics mine.

Epilogue

1. Faber, *Pilgrim Hymnal*, 369.

2. The title of this book is modeled on the title of a book written by my son, Richard H. Minear, *Hiroshima: Three Witnesses* (Princeton, N.J.: Princeton University Press, 1990). Reading *those* witnesses induced me to take more seriously their biblical predecessors.

3. Reliance on the Genesis stories of creation and fall is a basic characteristic of all three witnesses. In this respect this volume is a sequel to my earlier one, published under the title *Christians and the New Creation: Genesis Motifs in the New Testament* (Philadelphia: Westminster John Knox Press, 1994).

4. Anderson, *Imagined Communities*, 6.

5. Ibid., 10f.

Index of Scripture Readings